Everyday VOODOO

Beth Dolgner

4880 Lower Valley Road, Atglen, PA 19310

"Columns with Trees" ©Kathy Gold. Photo courtesy of BigStockPhoto.com

Designed by John P. Cheek
Type set in Aurora BdCn BT/New Baskerville BT

ISBN: 978-0-7643-3419-1
Printed in China

Schiffer Books are available at special discounts for bulk purchases for sales promotions or premiums. Special editions, including personalized covers, corporate imprints, and excerpts can be created in large quantities for special needs. For more information contact the publisher:

Published by Schiffer Publishing Ltd.
4880 Lower Valley Road
Atglen, PA 19310
Phone: (610) 593-1777; Fax: (610) 593-2002
E-mail: Info@schifferbooks.com

For the largest selection of fine reference books on this and related subjects, please visit our web site at **www.schifferbooks.com**
We are always looking for people to write books on new and related subjects. If you have an idea for a book please contact us at the above address.

This book may be purchased from the publisher.
Include $5.00 for shipping.
Please try your bookstore first.
You may write for a free catalog.

In Europe, Schiffer books are distributed by
Bushwood Books
6 Marksbury Ave.
Kew Gardens
Surrey TW9 4JF England
Phone: 44 (0) 20 8392-8585; Fax: 44 (0) 20 8392-9876
E-mail: info@bushwoodbooks.co.uk
Website: www.bushwoodbooks.co.uk

Contents

Dedication

For my mom, Ann.

Acknowledgments

I owe a big thanks to my editor, Dinah Roseberry, for her help and patience. I am also grateful to Peter Schiffer, who dreamed up the idea for *Everyday Voodoo*. I hope this book is a fitting tribute to his memory.

This book would not have been possible without the openness, kindness, and cooperation of the wonderful Voodoo practitioners who shared their stories and insight. In addition to those mentioned in these pages, I'd also like to thank Dora at Voodoo Authentica of New Orleans Cultural Center and Collection. Also, Claudia Williams and Jan Spacek of Starling Magickal deserve extra thanks for going above and beyond to help educate me in the ways of Voodoo.

Thanks to Mom for the editing help.

My husband Ed has been unyieldingly supportive, as always. And, as always, I am grateful.

INTRODUCTION
At the Crossroads

It all started with one sentence: "So, what do you know about Voodoo?" That short e-mail from my editor, Dinah, was what began my journey into Voodoo.

Coming into this project, the most I knew about Voodoo was that there are a lot of misconceptions about the religion. Sure, I'd popped into Voodoo shops during trips to New Orleans, but I'd never stopped to ask anyone what it was all about.

When you do stop to ask, though, you sure get a lot of answers. At its very core, Voodoo is a religion that honors one God and many spirits. These spirits, called orisha or loa, are intercessors between humans and God. Voodoo practitioners ask favors of the loa in exchange for honor and offerings. In addition to these divine spirits, the spirits of ancestors are also highly revered and can lend a spiritual hand when needed.

That is about where the common thread ends among the various types of Voodoo. In traditional Haitian Voodoo, rituals are performed with careful precision and people go through elaborate initiation ceremonies. In New Orleans, Voodoo is a more relaxed setting in which anyone can participate. For others, Voodoo is a solitary practice involving small altars built at home. Hoodoo is even further from the traditional roots, focusing on the magical aspect of Voodoo but downplaying the religious focus.

Many words are spelled differently depending on whom you ask; guidelines on how to build an altar vary widely. One mambo, or priestess, might conduct a ritual one way, while another has a different approach. The way *you* develop your rituals might be different from both of theirs.

And that's perfectly okay.

There is no right or wrong when it comes to practicing Voodoo. As long as you have pure intentions and respect for the spirits, it doesn't matter what words you use, whether you have a traditional altar, or even if you have never met a priest or priestess.

In conducting research for this book, I had the opportunity to speak with and meet a group of knowledgeable and kind people, from priestesses to shopkeepers and even a few strangers who brightened my trip to the cemetery in New Orleans. Although the traditions of each varied, they all stressed that Voodoo is a religion that everyone can practice, and you can create rituals and forge relationships with the loa in a way that speaks to you.

Voodoo is an everyday practice for many people, and it can be applied to everyday concerns. Whether it's a matter concerning your home (a sick loved one, the need for more money, protection) or your workplace (stopping gossip, sweetening up a co-worker, eliminating stress), you can use Voodoo to help you achieve your desires.

I have tried to be as accurate as possible with the information presented in these pages. When there are multiple views regarding a particular topic, I have tried to be fair in presenting all of the options available. During the Voodoo ritual I participated in with Priestess Claudia Williams of Starling Magickal, she spoke with the orisha Oshun on my behalf, asking for guidance so that my book would be an accurate representation of Voodoo. I hope I have achieved that. This book is only an introduction to the fascinating world of Voodoo, and the Recommended Reading list that I've included will help you further your knowledge.

Of all the Voodoo spirits that I learned about, Papa Legba is perhaps my favorite. He is the guardian of the crossroads, a teacher, and a trickster. When I received that one-sentence e-mail from Dinah, I was at a crossroads of my own. One possible path was to decline this book offer. After all, what did I know about Voodoo? Instead, I chose the other path, signing up for a journey down a road I'd never before traveled. It was a lot of work, it was a lot of learning, and it was a lot of fun. I hope Papa Legba is proud, and I hope your own journey down the Voodoo path is as rewarding as mine has been.

What Voodoo is Not

Before we even begin discussing what Voodoo is, let's take a look at what it is not. There are a lot of misconceptions about Voodoo that stem from ignorance and fear, and that ignorance and fear is present because, for many people, Voodoo is shrouded in mystery.

Don't feel bad about not knowing more about Voodoo already: Unless you personally know a Voodoo practitioner, it can be tough to track down information about the religion. I'm guessing there aren't a lot of Voodoo books in the religion section at your local book store. And let me tell you, of the books that are available, some of them could give you a headache because of their scholarly style. (Of course, the anthropologists who wrote those books weren't writing for me or the rest of the general public.)

Chances are you don't know much about Voodoo yet, and I want you to forget what little you have learned, because it's likely incorrect. You'll know you have received misinformation if any of your conceptions about Voodoo include the following words: evil, Satanic, outdated, scary, revenge, simple, unimportant, violent, or fake.

Black Magic

Despite what Hollywood might have you think, Voodoo is not a malevolent practice, nor is it Satanic (in fact, there is no Satan in Voodoo). Like many misunderstood religions, the black magic label has been tacked onto Voodoo because, to an outsider, some of the practices are unfamiliar and therefore intimidating.

Far from being black magic, Voodoo actually promotes goodwill. "When I am right, my magic will prevail" is an assuring statement Marie-José Alcide Saint-Lot recorded while visiting a Voodoo ritual. (Saint-Lot, 2003, 165) Of the thousands of rituals, most deal with positive magic: Health, protection, prosperity, and love are popular subjects for Voodoo spells, or "fixes." While it is possible to find negative fixes, you're not likely to encounter those easily. If you don't believe me, take a look at some of the online shops listed in the Voodoo directory at the back of this book. The products offered are all of a positive nature and aren't intended to be used for revenge or spite.

It is actually difficult to classify Voodoo spirits, called orisha and loa, as either good or evil. They all have defining characteristics but are morally ambivalent. It is the intent of the practitioner that is good or evil. Like any religion, there will be those who ask for help from the loa for dark purposes. On the whole, though, Voodoo promotes a sense of community and its rituals have a decidedly optimistic outlook.

Polytheistic

The spiritual plane is a crowded place in Voodoo, but that's not because it's packed with gods. Voodoo honors just one God, Bondye, who reigns supreme over both humans and the other divine entities.

Those others are spirits, called orisha or loa (as I mentioned earlier) depending on the Voodoo tradition, and there are thousands of them. The loa have human characteristics, and just like people, they have varying personalities, tastes, and physical appearances. The loa act as intercessors, carrying the requests of Voodoo practitioners to Bondye.

The relationship between believers, loa, and Bondye is very similar to the Catholic belief that the saints intercede on behalf of Christians. Some of the saints and loa are nearly interchangeable today, because Catholicism was the preferred religion of the white slave owners in Haiti. To make it look as though they were conforming to that religion, Voodoo practitioners adopted the names of Catholic saints to refer to the loa they resembled. For example, the loa associated with the snake, Damballah, became associated with St. Patrick, known for ridding Ireland of snakes. Over the years, the two religions have blended, and accoutrements of Catholic worship can be found in Voodoo rituals, and, in some cases, elements of Voodoo have been incorporated into Catholic services.

Nothing but "Magic"

If you've ever visited New Orleans, you've probably been drawn into one of the many Voodoo shops that dot the French Quarter. They're nearly impossible to resist, with Voodoo dolls, mojo bags, and unrecognizable items (Was that attached to an animal at one time?) hanging in the windows.

While this very visible side of Voodoo deals with magic, there's a lot more to the religion. "Besides the belief in the supernatural, Vodou stands for change, justice, freedom, brotherhood, which are all universal values vital to social cohesion and equilibrium." (Saint-Lot, 2003, 165)

In fact, Voodoo can be seen as the bond that holds many communities together. In rural temples, a farmer might sacrifice a goat to the

loa, but that goat will then feed others in the community. In many cases, pleasing the loa means serving the community. As you'll see in the next chapter, Voodoo can also give oppressed people the courage and unity needed to stand up for themselves.

A Simple, Quick Fix

Thousands of loa, complex rituals, long lists of objects for use in magic, offerings, altars...there is nothing simple about the structure of Voodoo. Nor is there anything quick about it. If you pick up a mojo bag that is intended for prosperity, don't expect to trip over a pile of money on your way out of the shop. The loa work at their own pace, and you'll just have to sit back, believe they are working for you, and be patient.

Anna, the priestess who owns Erzulie's in both New Orleans and Rhode Island, says that one of the biggest misconceptions about Voodoo is "that it's a cure-all, twenty-four-hour magic-bean fix. They forget, or they just don't know, that Voodoo is one of the most ancient, complicated, enriching, and holistic religions in the world. It is extremely complex. It isn't this "stick a pin in the Voodoo doll and get Johnny back," "stick a pin in and get your boss fired." That is so superficial and ridiculous. I think the Western—when I say Western, I mean more American—perception

of Voodoo is on the cusp of absurdity and carnival black magic workers."

It would take a very long book to try to explain everything about Voodoo. It would also be confusing to a newcomer and would probably result in the book collecting dust on a shelf after being shut in frustration. I think, though, this overview will give you a new appreciation for the depth of Voodoo.

A Voodoo doll by Madrina Angelique of Oshun's Botanica.

The History of Voodoo

"Now go do that Voodoo that you do so well!"
~Hedley Lamar, *Blazing Saddles*

Now that you know what Voodoo *isn't*, it's time to take a look at what Voodoo *is*. Voodoo, in its purest form, is a religion. Its practices and beliefs trace their origins to several West African tribes, though it has evolved over the centuries.

The West African peoples who contributed beliefs and rites to Voodoo include the Fon, Nago, Ibos, Congos, Dahomeans, Senegalese, Haoussars, Caplaous, Mandinges, Mondongues, Angolese, Libyans, Ethiopians, and Malgaches. It is the Fon people in what is now Benin, however, who get the most credit for contributions to Voodoo.

Although its roots come from West Africa, Voodoo is really a religion born of slavery. Spanish settlers brought the first African slaves to the island of Hispaniola in the early sixteenth century. That island eventually became known as Haiti, where Voodoo still flourishes today. The Spanish, French, and English brought slaves from Africa to the Caribbean, and Africans from different tribes found themselves working, sleeping, and worshipping together.

As the cultural lines blurred within Haiti's slave population, a new religion began to emerge: one that combined the most prominent aspects of various West African beliefs. New beliefs and rituals were added over time as the religion evolved. By the mid-1700s, Voodoo was firmly established as the religion that united the Africans enslaved in Haiti.

Slavery and Voodoo

Voodoo wasn't just something that united the African slaves in Haiti: it also became an outlet for their frustration and, ultimately, the empowerment they needed to secure their freedom.

In West Africa, where their ancestors had lived as free people, the gods they worshipped offered protection and balance. In a world where they were brutally treated and considered the property of their white owners, though, the old gods couldn't offer much assistance. The slaves were in need of something—or someone—that expressed their anger and frustration. Even more importantly, they were in need of something more powerful than their oppressors.

In answer to the slaves' needs, a new type of loa, or spirit, evolved: the petro loa. Petro loa are aggressive, fierce, and supportive of violent activity. Petro loa are balanced by rada loa, the spirits that represent protection and balance, much like the West African gods.

While petro loa and rada loa are very different in characteristics, they cannot be classified as either good or evil. They simply exist, and it is the Voodoo practitioner invoking their help who has either good or evil intentions.

Voodoo practitioners who favored petro loa were sometimes involved in a "petro cult," focusing their rituals on these violent spirits. The anger of many petro cultists finally boiled over, bringing about a slave revolt in Haiti. In 1804, Haiti was no longer a country of slaves and masters: The revolt transformed Haiti into a free country. In fact, Haiti was the second free colony in the western hemisphere. (Lovell, 2002, 217)

With their religion and their freedom so closely intertwined, it's easy to see why Voodoo grew in popularity throughout Haiti. It is still the prominent religion in Haiti, and it is found worldwide in other variations, such as Santeria.

Coming to America

As the practice of slavery increased in North America, so did the practice of Voodoo. Many slaves were brought to America from the French West Indies, where Voodoo already had a solid foothold. When Haiti became a free nation, many plantation owners fled to America with their slaves in tow, and Voodoo gained even more prominence in the growing country.

Many slaves entered America through Louisiana, but thousands also worked on plantations in Georgia, South Carolina, and other states. Communication among slaves was difficult for several reasons. White plantation owners rarely let slaves gather in large groups, let alone visit and communicate with slaves from neighboring plantations. The geography of the land didn't help, either: the bayous of Louisiana and the swampy low country areas of Georgia and South Carolina increased the isolation of the plantations.

New slaves arriving in America, though, brought with them their Voodoo practices, and the religion continued to grow. An important shift began in 1860. After that time, most slaves were actually born in North America. (Pinn, 2006, 223) The isolation of the plantation slaves coupled with the lack of new arrivals sparked an evolution in Voodoo.

According to New Orleans Voodoo historian Jerry Gandolfo, records of slaves brought to New Orleans indicate that they came directly from Africa to the French territory of Louisiana, so "New Orleans Voodoo" evolved very differently from the Haitian practice.

The oral tradition of Voodoo coupled with the isolation of slaves spread across the South further encouraged Voodoo's progression. The most prominent change was the growing loa pantheon: Spirits with desired characteristics were constantly introduced. Loa who had been immensely popular in Haiti fell out of vogue in America, and new loa emerged to take their places. The loa that practitioners on a plantation in Louisiana honored could be completely different from the loa celebrated by slaves in Georgia. Loa numbered in the thousands, and even today it is impossible to name them all.

Voodoo and Catholicism

Wary slave owners and government authorities sought to discourage the practice of Voodoo, going so far as to beat slaves who were caught worshipping the loa. Surely the Voodoo-fueled revolt in Haiti played a part in their fear of the religion. The more slave owners tried to suppress the practice, the tighter Voodoo practitioners clung to their religion. Instead of abandoning their beliefs, the slaves found ways to practice Voodoo in secret.

One of the most effective means of hiding Voodoo in the open was to adopt Catholic terminology. Many Voodoo practitioners were also practicing Catholics, the religion the plantation owners condoned. Even today, Catholic elements can still be found in Voodoo practices.

In some Voodoo traditions, the Psalms hold special magical properties.

Loa were associated with various Catholic saints. Voodoo practitioners knew that when they saw one of their own honoring the Catholic saints, that person was really paying tribute to the corresponding loa. The always-watchful slave owners, however, were none the wiser.

For example, St. Peter is the gatekeeper to Heaven, and he became associated with Papa Legba, the loa who is keeper of the crossroads where humans and loa interact. The female loa Yamaya, as a mother of a deity and a symbol of unconditional love, became the counterpart to the Virgin Mary. St. Patrick, known for driving the snakes out of Ireland, is tied to Damballah, the serpent loa.

In an ironic twist, a Catholic church in Port-Au-Prince, Haiti, recognized the power of Voodoo and incorporated it into their own worship services. The church adopted the use of drums and dancing used in Voodoo rituals to illustrate Biblical lessons. (Saint-Lot, 2003, 38)

Voodoo vs. Hoodoo

Voodoo evolved along several distinct paths. For some practitioners, the magical aspects of Voodoo took precedence: love charms, mojo bags, Voodoo dolls, and other fixes. In its extreme—with almost no emphasis on religion—is hoodoo.

Hoodoo doesn't have the religious focus associated with Voodoo, nor does it possess the same sense of community. Hoodoo is very much

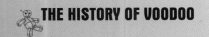

about the individual practitioner, who uses the magic of hoodoo for their own benefit. Also known as "Southern hoodoo," it is especially popular in the southern United States.

Styles of Voodoo

There are many variations of Voodoo and, in some cases, Voodoo practice falls somewhere between hoodoo and traditional Voodoo. Haitian Voodoo is the religion that many people think of first, picturing dancing, chanting, women wearing white dresses and turbans, and animal sacrifice. West African Voodoo is an even older version of Voodoo, where the African spirits, or orisha, are honored.

Santeria is popular in Cuba and South America, particularly Brazil, and many of its current practitioners hail from Latin American backgrounds. Santeria shares the same roots as Voodoo. It honors the orisha, too, but there are also elements of Catholicism and Native American practices present.

Other tenets of Voodoo are a mix of several styles, as well. New Orleans Voodoo is perhaps the best-known of these, blending Haitian Voodoo, hoodoo, Catholicism, and sometimes even Native American traditions. Jerry Gandolfo of the New Orleans Historic Voodoo Museum describes the city's brand of Voodoo as parochial and notes that the spirit of entrepreneurship is almost as important as the divine spirits.

The Voodoo rituals that were performed in Congo Square—a public space just outside the New Orleans French Quarter—on Sundays were so fascinating that people would come just to watch. Eventually, visitors could buy "souvenirs" to take with them, in the form of gris-gris bags, charms, and other items. That enterprising spirit is reflected today in the many Voodoo shops scattered throughout the French Quarter. The times may have changed, but tourism hasn't.

How Do You Spell It, Anyway?

Voodoo, vodou, voudou...there seem to be as many different spellings for "Voodoo" as there are loa! So which one is correct?

Believe it or not, all of them. Some scholars speculate that "Voodoo" derives from the word "vo-du." In the language of the Fon people of West Africa, vo-du means "god." (Pinn, 2006, 216) Claudia Williams of Starling Magickal suggests that the term derives from the French "voir dieu," which translates to "see God."

Whatever the origins of the word really are, we are still left with a handful of spellings today. Some people use the different spellings to refer to the different Voodoo practices: one to reference Haitian Voodoo, one for New Orleans Voodoo, and so forth. But to make things easier, we're just sticking with Voodoo throughout this book.

Recognition

In 1945, the World Order of Congregational Churches recognized what Voodoo practitioners already knew: that Voodoo is an official religion. Over 1,000 Voodoo temples were identified in Louisiana alone. (Pinn, 2006, 225)

With so many varying practices and thousands of loa, it is difficult to sum up Voodoo in a small space. Researcher Harold Coulander perhaps said it best:

> "Vodou is clearly more than the ritual of the cult temple. It is an integrated system of concepts concerning human behavior, the relation of mankind to those who have lived before, and the supernatural forces of the universe. It relates the living to the dead and those not yet born. It explains unpredictable events by showing them to be consistent with established principles. In short, it is a true religion which attempts to tie the unknown to the known and thus create order where chaos existed before." (Saint-Lot, 2003, 39)

Voodoo Divinity

The breakdown of Voodoo divinity is fairly simple: one god, called Bondye, rules over all. Below Bondye are the divine spirits, who act as intercessors between humans and Bondye.

In Haitian Voodoo, these spirits are called loa, or lwa (pronounced "l-WAH"). In African tradition, as well as Santeria and other paths, the spirits are known as orisha. A spirit in one tradition has its counterpart in the other. For example, Papa Legba is a loa, and his orisha counterpart is Elleggua. They share nearly identical characteristics and purposes.

While there are a finite number of orisha, there are, as said prior, thousands of loa, with more joining their ranks every day. The orisha tend to have broad specialties, such as love or money, whereas a loa often answers a very specific need, like getting the girl you had a crush on in high school to fall in love with you.

To further confuse things, some people use "loa" and "orisha" interchangeably, though most make a distinction between the two: Orisha originated in Africa and loa stem from Haitian Voodoo.

To simplify things, I'm using the term "loa" throughout this book to refer to the divine spirits of Voodoo as a whole.

Opinions vary about whether or not you can honor both loa and orisha, though ultimately the decision is yours. Brandi Kelley of Voodoo Authentica of New Orleans Cultural Center and Collection says all that matters is one thing: "What brings you closer to God and spirit?"

New Orleans Voodoo tends to embrace all beliefs. Brandi notes that you'll see altars in New Orleans that have African and Haitian statues, a Catholic saint, Native American totems, and even some Mardi Gras beads.

Some loa are popular throughout the world, while others are honored in only one Voodoo temple. The loa outlined in this chapter are typically the more popular ones, although a few obscure loa made it on the list thanks to unusual names or characteristics.

It's these characteristics that set the loa apart from each other. They can be physical or spiritual traits, and they can range from how a loa walks to what kinds of food it likes (sweets and alcohol, particularly rum, seem to be the favorites).

Estimates for the number of loa top 2,000, but there are probably thousands upon thousands more. We could never name them all, simply because we could never know them all. Because of Voodoo's isolated nature, some loa that are considered indispensable in one temple may not even be known to practitioners at another. Loa have also come in and out of vogue, and it's likely that some have been lost because no written account of their existence was ever made.

Similarly, the names of some loa have different spellings, while other loa have multiple incarnations, each with a different name. The loa Danballa might also be referred to as Damballah or Damballah Wedo, for example. The spellings listed in this book are the most common, but you might see different spellings and incarnations elsewhere.

A Day in the Life of a Loa

They might dwell in the spiritual plane, but the loa live very much like humans. They have spouses, are attached to families, and exhibit physical traits much like we do. And, more than anything, the loa love attention.

Serving the loa can result in good fortune and requests being granted, but the practitioner isn't the only one who benefits. The loa love to receive offerings and attention, though the mutually-beneficial service goes beyond that: If there were no humans, there would be no one to honor the loa. In that way, the loa are as dependent on us as we are on them, so keeping us safe and healthy is vitally important to the loa.

The loa act as the guardians of humans, always expecting to be properly honored for their intercession. If the humans to whom they have granted requests don't honor them properly, the loa are obliged to retaliate. They can bring illness, misfortune, and danger. (Lovell, 2002, 56)

The relationship is almost like that between a parent and a child. Since prosperity is a common request, we'll use that as our example. If a human calls on a loa to bring prosperity, promising an offering of rum in exchange, it's akin to a child asking a parent for, say, an allowance. The child might promise to sweep the floors in exchange for a couple of dollars.

Keys are sometimes left as offerings on altars.

When the floors aren't swept, though, the child hasn't upheld his end of the bargain. Not only will he not get his allowance, but he might be further punished by having to do more chores. In the same way, the practitioner who forgets that he owes his newfound prosperity to a loa will keenly regret it.

The loa might be strict in that sense, but at the same time they are very understanding. You may not know exactly what to say or what to offer to a loa, but that's okay. It's your intention that matters. If a particular loa loves expensive wine but that's too much for your budget, use a substitute. The loa will understand. It's only when you blow off your promise to honor the loa that you need to worry about trouble. If you're making the effort with an honest and grateful heart, the loa will let a few things slide.

Because of the close nature of the relationship between humans and the loa, it's okay to deal with them as if they are a revered friend. Speak to them as you would a friend, treat them with respect, and uphold your end of the bargain to show your gratitude.

Possession

When most of us hear the word "possession," we immediately picture scenes from the movie, *The Exorcist*. In the Christian tradition, possession is the work of demons and is a sign of the presence of evil. Hollywood took that image and stepped it up a notch, producing movies that bring to mind heads spinning on their necks and bodily functions I doubt any of us want to delve into right now.

Possession in the Voodoo tradition, however, is a very different thing. The spirits that practitioners revere—the loa—are the ones doing the possessing. Possession is not evil, although it may be a little unsettling at times depending on the severity and length of the loa's occupation inside a person.

Loa can be physically present at a Voodoo ceremony by entering a pottery jar called a govi or by possessing a follower. This act is called "mounting," and the practitioner who is possessed is called the "horse" or "cheval." The possession is so complete that the cheval acts unconsciously and will later remember none of what passed while he was possessed.

While possessed, a cheval will take on the physical movements associated with the loa who has mounted him. If someone is possessed by Papa Legba, then he may stoop over and move like an old man. If a woman is possessed by Erzulie, she will carry herself proudly like a confident, beautiful woman.

Even more important are the supernatural abilities chevals seem to take on when they are possessed. In her book, *Faces in the Smoke*, author

Douchan Gersi tells of witnessing acts that are generally thought impossible. She mentions standing at the back of a crowd watching a Voodoo ceremony. When the woman next to her became possessed, the woman rose into the air, flew over the heads of others, and landed in the middle of the ceremony.

Typically, a loa possesses someone for more practical purposes. Although a loa will occasionally possess someone in order to inflict punishment, staying inside a body so long that it is exhausted or even injured, it is far more common for a loa to give aid.

Some of the reasons a loa possesses a person include:

- For protection
- To pass along power in order to accomplish a task
- To offer advice
- To cure an illness in that person or others
- To warn of danger
- To receive offerings given by the possessed or other participants in the ceremony

(Rigaud, 1985, 49)

This last reason is especially interesting, because oftentimes liquor, such as rum, is included in the offerings left for a particular loa. There are numerous accounts of chevals gulping down full bottles of liquor. Normally, this would at least make a person sick, if not cause more serious consequences. During possession, though, the loa is the one imbibing the alcohol and the cheval feels no ill effects. Even after the loa has left the person, there are no signs of drunkenness.

Sometimes, the loa are having so much fun receiving attention and participating in the Voodoo ceremony that they don't want to leave the body they are possessing. In cases such as these, the houngan or mambo (Voodoo priest or priestess) can send them away so the cheval will once again be conscious and in control of himself.

Vèvès

Before we move on to a list of the loa, it's worth noting that in the past you wouldn't have been likely to see many physical representations of them, such as carvings or drawings. When Voodoo was still the religion of slaves, they wouldn't make anything representing the spirits because their owners would have punished them for having such a thing in their possession. It would have been physical proof that the slaves had their own religion

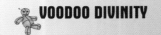

and were not, in fact, the devout Catholics they claimed to be. Physical representations are more common now than they once were, and you'll see pictures of Voodoo dolls representing loa throughout this book.

On the other hand, symbols called vèvès (pronounced "vay-vays") have long been used in ceremonies to attract the loa and their power. The vèvès help channel astral power and are often traced in powders such as flour or ashes. Each loa has a vèvè associated with it, so depending on the type of ceremony and which loa is being honored, the vèvès will be different.

Unlike statues or drawings, the vèvès could be brushed away following a ceremony. Today, vèvès are sometimes painted on altars or on the walls of a Voodoo temple. They appear in other unlikely places, too. During a trip to Key West when I was in college, I got a henna tattoo from a street artist. I picked a lovely stylized heart for the design, and it wasn't until I began doing research for this book that I realized I'd had the vèvè for Erzulie, the loa of beauty and love, painted onto my skin!

The vévé for Baron Samedi, drawn on a sidewalk in New Orleans.

God and the Spirits

The Seven African Powers

First and foremost, it is important to mention the Seven African Powers. These seven orisha are deities of the Yoruba people of Africa. Although the list of seven changes slightly from one belief system to another, they are, on the whole, a widely recognized group of divine beings. Because they are extremely powerful spirits, chances are many of your own works will be done in conjunction with these seven highly respected entities.

Inside Voodoo Authentica of New Orleans Cultural Center and Collection.

Though African in origin, the Seven African Powers are present in all Voodoo traditions, but the naming is sometimes slightly different. Because they are orishas, each of the seven has one or more corresponding loa. As mentioned before, the orisha Ellegua is known in Haitian and New Orleans Voodoo as the loa Legba, or Papa Legba.

The characteristics of each of the Seven African Powers can be found throughout the list of loa at the end of this chapter, but below are their names, with their Haitian Voodoo names and incarnations in parenthesis. In some cases, I have chosen to include both the African spirit and its Haitian counterpart in the list of loa. This is because the characteristics between them can vary so much that they are worth noting separately: Oya is a woman, but the Gede family that is associated with her is dominated by males. Oshun is just one entity, but Erzulie has several incarnations. The key is to choose the one with whom you feel the closest connection. The advantage of practicing Voodoo on your own is that you can honor the loa of your choosing, whether they hail from Africa, Haiti, or elsewhere.

The Seven African Powers and their Corresponding Loa

- Elleggua (Papa Legba)
- Obatala (Batala)
- Yemaya (La Sirene Balianne, Agwe)
- Oya (The Gedes, Baron Samedi)
- Oshun (Erzulie Freda)
- Chango (Damballah La Flambeau)
- Ogun (Ogu)

Honoring the Seven African Powers

Loa	Purpose	Colors	Day/Number	Offerings
Elleggua	Communication, removing obstacles	Red, black	Monday/3	Rum, candy
Obatala	Peace, balance, matters of the mind	White, silver, purple	Sunday/8	Black-eyed peas, coconuts
Yemaya	The home, women's affairs, motherhood	Blue, white, silver	Saturday/7	Cornmeal, molasses, watermelon
Oya	Ancestors, change, success	Red, purple, brown, orange	Wednesday/9	Red wine, grapes, eggplant
Oshun	Love, beauty, sex, relationships, art	Yellow, green, coral	Thursday/5	Honey, cinnamon, pumpkins, French pastries
Chango	Power, defeating enemies, strength	Red, white	Friday/6	Apples, yams, corn, peppers
Ogun	Protection, power, employment	Green, black	Tuesday/3 or 4	Nuts, berries, meat

Loa and their Characteristics

Bondye

Bondye is the supreme God. Like the God of Judeo-Christian and Muslim faiths, Bondye is the creator of the universe. The loa who serve Bondye are actually manifestations of him, so their existence is dependent upon Bondye. (Pinn, 2006, 219) This relationship is similar to the Christian holy trinity, in which God, Christ, and the Holy Spirit are separate entities, yet still God himself.

Voodoo tradition says that after Bondye created the universe, he was ready for a well-deserved break. He retired, so to speak, assigning the loa to be his earthly ambassadors.

Aida Wedo/Ayizan

The rainbow represents Ayizan, but her physical appearance is that of an old woman, bent as if from years of hard work. She might be represented as elderly, but Ayizan has the privilege of being the wife of Damballah, one of the most important loa in Voodoo.

Aida Wedo's help is sought for protection, fertility, and blessings.

Chango

Chango is a strong loa, repre-senting fire, thunder, power, and sensuality. He is the loa you need to approach for strength, when you need help defeating your enemies, or to gain power. With so much power at his disposal, it's not surprising that Chango is considered to have once been a king.

Red and white are the colors that should be used to decorate Chango's altar, and acceptable offerings for him include brightly-colored fruits and vegetables such as apples, yams, corn, and peppers.

Many loa are only associated with one Catholic saint, but Chango is actually related to two. His "saintly stand-ins" include both St. Barbara and St. Jerome.

Damballah

Damballah dominates the sky and is a symbol of purity. Because of this, the color associated with him is white. While extremely powerful, Damballah is known as a generous loa. Damballah's help is sought by people seek-ing wealth, happiness, and pure minds.

Also called Danballa and Damballah Wedo, he is one of the most popular and powerful loa in Voodoo. In the past, Damballah was typically honored with offerings of snakes or snake eggs, and he is represented by the snake. Today, foods that are more readily available are typically substituted. White food offerings are popular with Damballah, such as corn flour, champagne, pastries on white plates, an egg on a white saucer, white wine, or white sweets.

Damballah's Catholic counterpart is St. Patrick, who drove the snakes out of Ireland.

Elleggua/Papa Legba

In the divine pecking order, Papa Legba is the patriarch of all other loa. This oldest of loa might be a bent old man, but he is the most powerful. Legba is the intermediary between the loa and humans. If you want to reach Bondye through a loa, you have to convince Legba to let you talk to that loa in the first place. And if Legba says no, well, better luck next time.

Fortunately, Legba rarely says no. According to everyone I interviewed for this book, he responds easily and agreeably to anyone genuinely asking for his intercession (and paying him the proper respects, of course).

Voodoo rituals, both large gatherings in temples and solitary ones practiced at a home altar, always begin by honoring Legba and asking him to open the lines of communication with the other loa.

As the loa who opens the doorway between the physical and spiritual worlds, Legba is the master of doorways and crossroads. The crossroads are his domain, so if you have ever visited a country crossroads at midnight in hopes of dealing with the devil, chances are it was Legba you really needed to invoke. Blues legend Robert Johnson found that out, but more on that later.

Legba's status also makes him a symbolic gatekeeper, granting access to the world of the spirits. Because of this, his Catholic contemporary is St. Peter, who stands guard at the gates of Heaven.

Preferred offerings to Legba include rum, sweets, and tobacco. In addition to minding the crossroads of the physical and spiritual planes, you can also go to him for clarity of mind when facing difficult decisions or obstacles. When you are at a crossroads in your life, he can help you choose your path.

Red is Legba's favorite color, and his nickname is "Trickster." The image of an old man with a straw hat, a cane, and a sack slung over his back might not be intimidating, but Legba is a powerful loa who demands respect and recognition.

When you try the spells and rituals listed in this book, remember to ask for Legba's permission to interact with the loa of your choice before you begin. Chances are good he'll say yes.

An altar to Papa Legba at Starling Magickal.

Erzulie

Erzulie, a name often used by itself, is also the first name of a number of loa, including Erzulie Freda and Erzulie Dantor. There is also a third counterpart, known as La Sirene. These feminine love loa are not just about falling in love: They are also about loving oneself.

All three incarnations of Erzulie represent love, art, and sex, but they have significant differences in how they personify those things. Erzulie Freda is a very popular and cherished loa. In fact, a sign of her status and reverence is evident in that the Virgin Mary is her Catholic counterpart. Erzulie Freda helps find a lover and she can restore the spark to a relationship that has fizzled. This love loa is such a symbol of goodness and beauty that her presence can counteract evil magic. To further add to her allure, Erzulie Freda can also grant wealth and opulent finery to her followers.

Erzulie Freda loves offerings of perfume, jewelry, and other beautiful objects. Although her beauty can lead to vanity, she is also generous because she loves to see beauty all around her. Erzulie Freda's physical appearance is represented by a pink dress and turban, three rings, bracelets, and earrings. Really, though, any finery can represent this loa associated with beauty and love. Her colors are blue and pink.

On the opposite side of the love spectrum, Erzulie Dantor embodies jealousy and passion. She is the patron loa of New Orleans, and a favorite loa for women who are victims of domestic abuse. Erzulie Dantor loves women with her characteristic passion (making her the favored loa of lesbians), but her love isn't a sexual one: She is a protector of women. As a mother herself, Erzulie Dantor is also passionately protective of children.

In addition to her protective services, Erzulie Dantor also helps women who have been crossed by a lover, independent women, and women who need help with financial matters.

Le Sirene is the third incarnation of Erzulie, and she represents another important aspect of female divinity: motherhood. In addition, La Sirene represents the sea, and she is closely connected to Yemaya (guardian of the sea).

Gede

Gede is the name often used to refer to Gede Nibo, but in reality there is an entire Gede family. They are the rulers of the dead and of cemeteries. Because the cemetery is the symbolic home of the Gede family, offerings to these loa are often left in cemeteries. Cemetery dirt can also be a valuable tool in working Voodoo magic.

Baron Samedi is the head of the Gede family and guardian of the cemetery. His symbol is a cross, and he is the keeper of the knowledge of the dead. He also controls the journey between life and death. Therefore, Baron Samedi is an important loa to invoke to ensure safe passage for deceased family and loved ones. Prayers are sent to the Baron for healing sick children and ill people who are near death.

The Baron wears a black tuxedo and a top hat, or just black slacks and a black shirt. He wears spectacles, too, and has a very white face. Practitioners sometimes dress as him during Voodoo rituals, painting their faces a deathly pallor and donning the glasses and black clothing.

The Gede family includes Papa Gede, who is the New Orleans counterpart to Baron Samedi. They share similar characteristics, and Papa Gede is also the lord of the cemetery.

As for Gede Nibo, he is characterized by raunchy, outlandish behavior, but he usually gets a laugh out of his audience. He is obsessed with sex, and he represents sexuality and fertility. A favorite among practitioners, Gede Nibo is most celebrated in November. It is interesting to note that a loa who hails from the cemetery is celebrated at about the same time as Halloween and Samhain, when the dead are believed to return to earth for one night.

Baron Samedi is married to Manman Brigit, the mother of cemeteries and a spirit of death. Usually depicted as a white woman, she is related to Ireland's St. Brigit. Manman Brigit is very sexual and, often, very crass. A fiery woman, she likes her rum offerings laced with hot peppers.

Gran Bois

Gran Bois translates to "big wood," a fitting term for the loa who oversees the sacred forest and the Island Below the Waters, which is home to the loa. The island is also the spiritual world to which the deceased must travel. St. Christopher is the patron saint of travelers, and so he shares an identity with Gran Bois.

Thanks to his status over the forest, Gran Bois protects animals and understands the healing powers of herbs. He can provide knowledge and healing to those who ask him for it. Green and white are preferred colors to use on his altar, and offerings should come from the forest: leaves, herbs, and flowers. He also likes food such as yams and bananas, and of course, Gran Bois is a fan of the ever-popular rum.

Loko

As the ruler of the forests, Loko has a vast knowledge of plants. Thanks to that knowledge, he is known as a healer and the overseer of agriculture. Loko, or Papa Loko, is symbolized by things often found in a forest: a tree, a butterfly, or a chameleon. He is even embodied by the wind. Not surprisingly, Loko's favored colors are green and yellow.

Marasa Twins

The Marasa Twins symbolize childhood, and they themselves are children. However, don't let their appearance fool you: If these loa don't receive the honor that is their due, they won't hesitate to punish the lax practitioner.

Fortunately, satiating the needs of the Marasa Twins isn't difficult. Like most children, they prefer sweets when it comes to offerings: popcorn, candy, cookies, or other treats. Just make sure you place their offering on the ground in front of the altar so it will be within reach of these child-like twins.

Obatala

A powerful spirit, the Yoruba people consider Obatala to be the supreme deity and creator of our existence. Obatala is ambiguous, encompassing both sides of everything: man/woman, beautiful/ugly, benevolent/vengeful. Obatala can restore the fallen to places of honor, but at the same time he can humble the arrogant.

Obatala restores peace and balance, solves problems, brings clarity, and is said to even cure cancer. Decorate Obatala's altar in white, silver, and purple, and leave offerings such as black-eyed peas and coconuts.

Obatala is associated with eggs and, particularly, with snakes. Like a constrictor, Obatala will spiritually "squeeze" a problem in order to eke out all of the knowledge about it. For this reason, Obatala can be a great asset when you are trying to make a serious decision and need to weigh all of your options.

Ogun

The color red denotes Ogun, the loa of warfare, political power, and protection. Ogun (also spelled Ogoun) wears blue pants and a red shirt, and he always carries a machete with him. He can be a powerful force for driving out evil influence and protecting the

practitioners who go to him for shelter. St. James is the saint linked to Ogun.

Ogun serves many purposes in addition to war and politics. He is also the loa who assists with hunting, metals, and the unemployed. If you're seeking the help of the loa to find a job, Ogun might be the one to ask.

Ogun's colors are green and black, and he loves simple offerings, including nuts, berries, and meat.

Oshun

Oshun is the loa of love, art, and dance. Practitioners go to her when they are seeking advice and favors in the areas of money, love, creativity, beauty, and laughter. Oshun is able to develop emotions, so she is also the loa to seek out if you need emotional strength.

Oshun's favorite offerings are gold and objects that have a golden shade: pumpkins, oranges, honey, cinnamon. She also appreciates mirrors and pastries. Surprisingly, Oshun's favorite color is not gold. Instead, she likes yellow, green, and coral.

Because the loa are seen as living very human lives, they enter into relationships and have children in a similar way. Oshun is married to Chango, and her son is Papa Legba.

Oya

Also known as Oya-Yansa, this queenly spirit helps you connect with your ancestors, and she assists in matters of business and change. If you ask her for change, make sure you really mean it: She tends to bring dramatic change that can really shake up your life!

Oya is a fierce woman, and although she is connected to death and cemeteries (her Haitian counterparts are the Gede family, including Baron Samedi), she will fight to transform your life, if you ask it of her.

Red, purple, brown, and orange are Oya's preferred colors, and offerings for her include things that reflect those hues: give her red wine, grapes, or eggplant.

Yemaya

Yemaya is the guardian of the sea, and her colors are blue, white and silver. She has domain over the home and women's affairs, and she also protects unborn children. If you seek her help, offer cornmeal, molasses or watermelon to her.

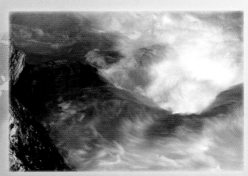

Zaka

Zaka is the loa of agriculture, an important spirit to anyone who farms or grows their own food, be it a few acres or a few tomato plants. Associated with St. John the Baptist, Zaka's colors are blue, red, and green.

Also known as Cousin Zaka, this loa is personified as a farm laborer, certainly someone with whom the slaves in Haiti and America found a kinship. Zaka's appearance is that of a peasant. He wears worn blue denim pants with one leg longer than the other, a denim shirt and a straw hat. To further his peasant appearance, the friendly loa also carries a knapsack, often made of a handkerchief.

Honorable Mentions

Some loa are worth noting here because of their interesting names and backstories. When it comes to unusual monikers, loa such as Captain Zombi, Papa Pierre, and Captain Debas are definitely on the list.

Proving that loa come in all shapes and sizes is the example of Simalo. When Antoine Simon was President of Haiti from 1908-1911, he declared that his goat was, in fact, the incarnation of a loa named Simalo.

Voodoo provides loa for all aspects of life and the world around us. Some loa have huge domains, such as Damballah and his heavenly abode in the skies. Others, such as Simbi, have smaller but no less important territory: Simbi is the guardian of ponds.

Don't Forget the Ancestors

The loa aren't the only spiritual beings who need attention and honor. In Voodoo tradition, the spirits of the ancestors become like loa themselves. One benefit of serving our ancestors is that the fear and unfamiliarity of working with spirits is dispelled. Priestess Luisah Teish says, "Through ancestor reverence we erase the 'Exorcist' tapes and learn to relate to spirits as friends, as members of the family." (Teish, 1985, xi)

Ancestors are considered a powerful source of protection and knowledge, and they can be called on for assistance. However, like the loa, the ancestral spirits need to receive due attention and honor. When it comes to making offerings to our ancestors, it's easy to know what to give them: they enjoy the same treats they did in life, whether it be jewelry, sweets, drinks, or a favorite delicacy.

As you honor those who went before you, remember that someday, your descendants may be calling on you, remembering your name and asking for your intercession. Show your ancestors the same respect that you would want shown to you.

Who's Who and What's What

"You remind me of the babe...The babe with the power...The power of Voodoo."

~David Bowie, *Labyrinth*

What's a houngan? Is a peristyle like a periscope? There are a lot of titles and terms in Voodoo, and it's easy to feel a little overwhelmed by them. Many of the unfamiliar words are used to describe players and aspects in formal Haitian Voodoo rituals, but some are important for even the individual practitioner to know.

The Leaders

Each Voodoo temple is led by a priest or priestess, but some of those leaders go by other titles. The traditional word for a Voodoo priest is "houngan," while a priestess is known as a "mambo." Some contemporary priestesses prefer terms like "mama" that reflect the role of the priestess: leading and caring for those in her temple.

The role of the priest or priestess is a difficult one, and many speak of the sacrifices that must be made in order to lead a Voodoo temple. An "ordinary" life is out of the question: The life of a houngan or mambo is dedicated to the loa and the people serving them. Because the houngan channels the energy of the loa during a ritual, the ceremonies are often physically, emotionally, and psychically exhausting. If a member of the temple is having a crisis, the mambo is there to serve, no matter the time. It's not a forty-hour-a-week job. Rather, it's a lifestyle commitment that takes years of training, initiation, and lifelong learning.

The symbol of a houngan or mambo is a rattle called an asson. The asson is given to the new priest or priestess during an intricate, and often lengthy, initiation. Rites of initiation vary between branches of Voodoo, and even from temple to temple.

In some temples, a ceremony to induct a new temple leader in the Haitian Voodoo tradition will be officiated by the existing houngan (or mambo), and he will be assisted by two other houngans. The initiate will be isolated for a period of time as a means of purification, and the amount of time the initiate is sequestered can vary greatly. During the ceremony itself, the elder houngan calls on each loa, and at the end of the ceremony, the initiate is possessed by a loa prior to accepting the asson. (Rigaud, 1985, 37)

The Members of a Temple

A typical Voodoo temple is much like a small community in which everyone has a certain job to perform. In addition to the houngan or mambo, there are a myriad of responsibilities that must be undertaken in order to have a successful ceremony.

Drumming is an important aspect of any ceremony, and the drummers are traditionally called "houn'torguiers." In temples that practice animal sacrifice (typically Haiti and Africa, where the animal will be used as food), the "houn'sih ventailleur" secures the animals, while the "houn'sih cuisiniere" handles the cooking of that animal following the ceremony.

Someone is even assigned the job of making sure everyone stays orderly. Called the "reine silence," this person ensures that everyone is respectful during each ritual.

The members of a Voodoo temple are called "hounsis." Tradition-ally, hounsis wear all white for rituals. The women don a white dress and head wrap, while men wear a white shirt and pants. An exception to this rule is that, sometimes, hounsis will wear the colors of the loa they are honoring at the time. While white garb is still used in Haiti, the dress code for rituals in other Voodoo traditions is more lax.

The Setting

As an individual practitioner, your rituals will be centered around your altar. In New Orleans Voodoo, a ritual might take place in a courtyard (as did the one in which I participated) or even inside a Voodoo shop. Some of the aspects of a traditional Voodoo temple are seen in even the non-traditional settings.

A temple is called an "oum'phor." In the center is a large area called the "peristyle," where the rituals actually take place. The ground of the peristyle will usually be covered with drawings or tracings in the sand of vévés, the symbols associated with the loa.

A "poteau-mitan" stands at the center of the peristyle and is typically a post reaching toward the sky, symbolizing the link between humans and the divine. That link is possible because of Papa Legba, so the poteau-mitan also represents him. Often, the post is painted with images of Damballah and Aida Wedo. (Rigaud, 1985, 16)

An altar standing about chest-high is located inside the peristyle. Called a "pé," the altar holds an array of objects, including offerings, decorations to please the loa, and items to be used during the ritual.

Trees also play an important role in a temple setting. Formally called "reposoirs," the trees are the dwelling places of loa. Each loa will have its own tree in which it likes to abide, so the trees are considered divine. If someone has an offering for a particular loa, they can leave it at the trunk of the tree belonging to that spirit.

A low wall usually surrounds the peristyle, allowing observers to watch while maintaining a separation from the actual ritual being performed within the sacred space.

The Importance of Drums

A traditional Voodoo ritual includes chanting, singing, dancing, and drumming. Although all of these aspects are important, perhaps none is so powerful as drumming. Drums help set the pace of the entire ritual, and they are used to build and channel energy. The pulsating sound of drums can help initiate possessions, and they enhance the link between the ritual participants and the spirits.

Drums are considered so vital that they are often treated as sacred objects. They are meticulously cared for and are even stored on grass "beds" so they can rest and recharge their psychic energy following a ritual.

What About Animal Sacrifice?

If you want to practice Voodoo, that doesn't mean you're going to need to sacrifice an animal. (Yes, I breathed a sigh of relief when I learned that, too.) Today, many of us buy our meat neatly packaged from the grocery store. In the past, and in many rural villages today, animals raised on small family farms provided nourishment.

In addition to serving the spiritual needs of its people, Voodoo also served the community's physical needs. Someone who donated an animal to be sacrificed wasn't just giving an offering to the spirits: He was feeding his family and neighbors. The whole animal would be put to use, with the skin used to make leather, the bones fashioned into useful tools and other parts used for magical purposes. Brandi Kelley of Voodoo Authentica of New Orleans Cultural Center and Collection notes that animals wouldn't be used after a sacrifice in only one instance: if the animal was used for drawing an illness out of someone. If that occurred, the animal would be considered tainted and unfit for consumption.

Because most temples don't need to provide food for their members today, animal sacrifice is far less common than it once was. Sacrificing an animal that won't be utilized is wasteful and impractical. Remember, Voodoo flourished under the guidance of people who were slaves and had very little to call their own. Neither they nor the loa believed in needless waste, and neither should we.

I Participate in a Voodoo Ritual

When Priestess Claudia Williams of Starling Magickal in New Orleans asked me if I wanted to participate in a Voodoo ritual, I immediately answered in the affirmative. My mother and I stumbled upon her occult shop in the French Quarter many years ago during my first trip to the city, and I've made a point of stopping by on every subsequent visit. Starling is a wonderful mix of Voodoo altars, occult accoutrements, rare books, and floor-to-ceiling shelves crammed with hand-labeled bottles. There is a warmth to the shop, which is located in a French Quarter house dating from the 1840s.

Claudia herself is a dynamic woman, full of energy, knowledge, and sass. She's one of the Voodoo practitioners profiled later in "Voodoo Today," and her path to priestesshood is a fascinating one. When I showed up at the shop prior to the ritual, Claudia immediately greeted me with a smile and a hug. I admit I was a little nervous about the ritual—largely because I just didn't know what to expect—but right then I knew I was in safe hands.

The courtyards of the New Orleans French Quarter are like hundreds of tiny hidden worlds offering refuge from the heat and noise on the streets. Behind the building that houses Starling is a courtyard, and behind that is a two-story building that once housed slaves. Beyond that is a second courtyard filled with lush vegetation, a fountain, and an altar: the home of the Temple of the Altar-Native Star. A high windowless wall rises on one side and a derelict house stands darkly on the other. I felt like we'd left the busy French Quarter altogether: Even though it was only a little after eight o'clock on a Friday night, it was silent and dark in the courtyard.

In the courtyard, a brick and concrete altar sat at one side, and the fountain sitting in the middle of the courtyard-cum-peristyle served as the poteau-mitan. The altar was decorated with clusters of candles and branches of ginger blossoms cut from a nearby tree.

Claudia's husband, Jan Spacek, positioned himself near the altar with a drum. His light drumming would provide the soundtrack for the whole experience, as he allowed the energy of the ritual to dictate his cadences.

The altar in the courtyard behind Starling Magickal.

Our ritual would be for prosperity (we writers need all the help we can get!), and therefore Oshun was the loa around whom our ritual would revolve. But first, Papa Legba had to give his permission and open the doorway between us and Oshun.

I'd brought along a bottle of rum as an offering for Legba and Oshun. I handed it to Claudia, and she stepped into the peristyle. Meanwhile, I sat just outside the two steps leading down onto the brick courtyard, the symbolic doorway through which I needed permission to enter.

Claudia gave Papa Legba her ritual greeting in French, then began speaking in a conversational, yet reverent, tone to him. She implored him to open the door, but she also took time to introduce me to him, explaining that I had never witnessed a Voodoo ritual before, and that I was writing a book about the religion. "She's brought you this offering of rum," Claudia explained further, holding the bottle aloft.

41

Claudia then proceeded to each of the four corners, or cardinal directions. At each she gave a brief greeting to the spirits before taking a swig of the rum and spraying it through her teeth, sending a fine mist through the air. This symbolic act of burning away negative energy with the rum would be repeated many times during the ritual.

Priestess Claudia Williams speaks to Papa Legba while her snake, Baron, rests around her neck.

Finally, I was able to enter the peristyle, as Claudia took me by the hand and led me down the steps and up to the altar. There, she went through another rum-spraying ritual, sending tiny droplets into the air on either side of my head and down near my feet. As she proceeded, she asked Oshun for her blessings in granting me prosperity and success.

I was given an African Trading Bead that carried the blessings bestowed in the ritual. The beautiful black bead is estimated to be between two- and four-hundred years old, and beads like it were used as currency and rewards in Africa for many years. The bead is now on a necklace, so I can keep it close and be reminded of the ritual and of the blessings that Claudia asked Oshun for on my behalf.

Before the part of the ritual that focused on me was complete, Claudia sprayed generous amounts of Florida Water in the air around me. Florida Water is much like holy water in Voodoo tradition and is used in much the same way. It cleanses, enhances energy, and beautifies the ceremony with its light floral scent.

Finally, Claudia thanked Oshun and Papa Legba, pouring some of the remaining rum onto the altar and ground for them. The remainder of the bottle was placed on the altar, and after the ritual formally ended I poured out the rest myself in thanks to the loa.

Far from being scary or strange, the entire ritual was actually very uplifting. When I stopped by Starling the next day, I described it to Jan as creating a feeling of peace and contentment. And because Starling's temple, the Temple of the Altar-Native Star, is a learning one, Claudia explained each part of the ritual to me throughout the process, so I was never left wondering why she did or said anything in particular.

Interestingly, there was only one time during the ritual when I didn't have that contented feeling. At one point, as I was gazing straight ahead, I saw a bright white point of light that appeared on my left, in the far edge of my vision. The light looked like it was moving over the fountain, but when I turned my head it disappeared. Immediately after seeing this, I was overcome with emotion and very nearly burst into tears. I wasn't sad, just overwhelmed. The light looked just like something I'd seen on a paranormal investigation, so is it possible a spirit was attracted to the energy of our ritual? Perhaps I'd tapped into the emotions of the spirit, hence my sudden urge to cry.

Whatever the explanation, there was definitely a palpable energy in the courtyard. Jan and Claudia both felt the spiritual charge in the air, but the most interesting confirmation of it came several days later. A friend of theirs paid a visit and mentioned to Claudia that he could feel energy in the place. He doesn't practice Voodoo and isn't a spiritual person by nature, but even he could sense the impact of the ritual.

If you're ever in New Orleans, call or stop by Starling to find out if the Temple of the Altar-Native Star will be hosting one of their free and open-to-all rituals. It's an incredible experience and will doubtless be one of the highlights of your visit. And, of course, my gratitude goes out to Claudia and Jan for their openness and kindness.

Voodoo Today

Modern Voodoo encompasses a wide range of practices, people, and places. While some people choose traditional Voodoo, going through initiations at a temple, others prefer more informal rituals or even solitary practice.

Voodoo can be found everywhere in the United States, but there are several areas where the culture is especially prolific. Brooklyn, New York, has a very active Voodoo population, thanks in part to local priestess Mama Lola, probably one of the best known mambos today. In addition to New Orleans, Southern cities where Voodoo can be found include Savannah, Georgia, and Miami, Florida, which has a large Haitian population. California is a haven for both Voodoo and Santeria practitioners, with many devout followers in Los Angeles and the San Francisco area.

While Voodoo was once shrouded in mystery by necessity, today's practitioners are often eager to educate others about their beliefs and rituals. Events like the annual Voodoofest in New Orleans open the world of Voodoo to newcomers, encouraging questions and interaction.

There is a lot to be learned, but ultimately, the spiritual path you choose is a very personal journey. Everyone I interviewed for this book had something in their lives that determined their spiritual path, and no two reasons for choosing Voodoo were the same. The priestesses profiled here have wonderful stories to share, and if you ever have the opportunity to meet a mambo or houngan, don't hesitate to ask them what inspired them to dedicate their lives to Voodoo.

Voodoofest

Voodoofest, just like New Orleans Voodoo, got its start in the storied Congo Square, where slaves once gathered every Sunday to perform rituals. Modern-day practitioners used to gather each Halloween to honor their ancestors in a public ritual. Finally, the decision was made to turn the annual event into a day of demonstrations and learning. Voodoofest was born.

First held in 1999, Voodoofest is a way to educate people about Voodoo while imparting information about its impact on New Orleans culture. On October 31st of each year, the 600 block of Rue Dumaine is blocked off, and Voodoo spills onto the street in front of Voodoo Authentica of New Orleans Cultural Center and Collection. The day-long event includes music, rituals, demonstrations, discussions, food, and even some audience participation.

In addition to offering a glimpse of real Voodoo, the festival also highlights the cultural contributions of the religion. Musicians talk about how Voodoo has influenced their music, and the food also reflects a Voodoo heritage.

Voodoofest organizer Brandi Kelley, who also owns Voodoo Authentica, feels that educating people about Voodoo is a vital need. When asked about misconceptions people have regarding Voodoo, she is quick to begin listing false assumptions.

People believe "that Voodoo is of the devil, ruled by Satan. There is no Satan in Voodoo!" Brandi says. She also notes that Voodoo dolls are often thought to be negative, when in fact the opposite is true. "What people fail to realize is that dolls and effigies are an ancient form of sympathetic magic. You don't see people doing all these hexes; they're very responsible about their magic. The doll is used primarily as a healing tool."

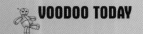

With so many misconceptions, it's easy to understand why Brandi feels that the hard work involved in Voodoofest (she spends days just preparing the food) is well worth it. Her message to people who want to practice Voodoo is that their magic should be positive. "First and foremost, use your magic responsibly," she advises. "If you are motivated by power, or wanting control over others, you'll learn that it's really about service to the spirits and service to others. It involves a lot of sacrifice."

Voodoofest is a free event, and everyone is welcome–especially those who attend in spiritual form. Ultimately, Voodoofest is a celebration of the ancestors, a chance for their spirits to bask in the honor and attention bestowed on them all day. Voodoofest always ends with a ceremony honoring the ancestors, and Brandi says that the day of demonstrations and learning is a fitting tribute to them. "It's all integrated and I think it really sends a message of acknowledgement to the ancestors, and to Voodoo," she says.

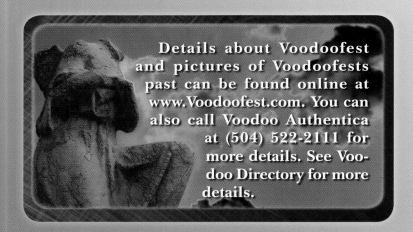

Details about Voodoofest and pictures of Voodoofests past can be found online at www.Voodoofest.com. You can also call Voodoo Authentica at (504) 522-2111 for more details. See Voodoo Directory for more details.

Madrina Angelique

When I asked the owner of Oshun's Botanica near Atlanta, Georgia, what title she prefers, she answered, "Madrina Angelique." Madrina means "mother" and is a reflection of the sense of family and care that goes into being a leader in the Voodoo community.

Angelique handcrafts beautiful dolls, wangas, mojo bags, and other Voodoo items. She offers Tarot card readings, as well, while one of her godsons reads cowrie shells—arguably one of the most difficult forms of divination, and one that takes lengthy study.

Rather than practicing traditional Voodoo, Madrina Angelique specializes in Southern hoodoo. This interesting blend of Voodoo and folk magic is alive and well in Georgia, and Angelique has tapped into the power of herb lore and magic.

A Voodoo fetish by Madrina Angelique of Oshun's Botanica.

How did you get into Voodoo and hoodoo?

It was just something that started when I was real young. I always had an interest in it from as long as I can remember. As a little girl I saw the Baron [Samedi] dance in front of my door. I must have been about two or three, and I remember getting a whipping for lying. I didn't know who he was until years later when I was in the library and I saw him in a book and I said, "There he is. That's who I saw!"

Did you have exposure to Voodoo while growing up?

When I was fifteen or sixteen I started seeking out people, which was very hard in the seventies because it wasn't as acceptable as it is now.

What are the major differences between Voodoo and hoodoo?

Hoodoo is a practice. It involves herbs, roots, offerings to nature, that kind of thing. Then there's New Orleans-style Voodoo, which is a mixture of hoodoo and Haitian Voodoo. Haitian Voodoo is a religion. [Hoodoo is] the practice of manipulating the universe to get what you want.

What are the biggest misconceptions about hoodoo?

That it's dark, that it's evil, that only "witches" practice it. It's basically just folk magic. You see the same thing in Appalachia; you see the same thing in most cultures.

For the individual practitioner, do they need to be initiated before using spells, gris-gris bags, and other works?

Those are things that I think can be accessed by anyone. I don't think the loa or the orisha are for a select few. Some people out there think you have to have an initiation to do things, and I don't believe that at all. I don't believe that they [the loa] will only respond to the "chosen ones." I think it's for everyone.

What advice do you have for new practitioners?

Learn your herbs. If you're going to put herbs in a bag and you want a love bag, learn which herbs go with love and which ones you respond to best. I can do the work for you, but I really don't care if your man comes back or not. I'll do the work for you and I'll work very hard, but you're the one that wants him so bad, so you're going to put a whole lot more energy into it.

What are the most common questions you receive?

Mostly it's misconceptions that they've gotten from TV. "Can I kill someone?" "Can I make this man love me?" If it's not meant to be,

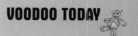

he's not going to love you, no matter how much work you do! You can't change what has already been pre-determined.

If that's the case, then what is the value of using this magic?

Removing obstacles. If he loves you but he lives clear across the country and he has no job here, you might be able to manipulate the universe to offer him a job that allows him to move closer to you.

You use a lot of found objects in your work. How do you choose what items to use?

I don't like to make things assembly-line. If you're going to make a mojo bag, traditionally it would be made of red felt, or red suede. That was traditional, but a lot of times that was because it was all they could get. Poor black people in New Orleans one hundred years ago, they couldn't get red satin. But if you feel the need to make your bag out of red satin, it's perfectly fine.

What do you consider essential to your practice?

Honesty. If people contact me and they are having problems, the first thing I do is give them something to do for themselves. We see if they can handle the situation themselves instead of telling them they need a hundred dollars' worth of my candles and a hundred dollars' worth of my baths and two-hundred dollars' worth of my Ellegbas. Let's see if you can take care of it yourself. If not, then I'll help you.

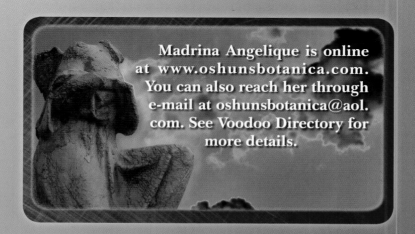

Madrina Angelique is online at www.oshunsbotanica.com. You can also reach her through e-mail at oshunsbotanica@aol.com. See Voodoo Directory for more details.

Claudia Williams

Claudia Williams has many titles: Reverend, High Priestess or simply Mama. The owner of Starling Magickal in New Orleans, Claudia has a wealth of knowledge about many occult paths. She is a Voodoo priestess as well as a psychic.

Starling sells a wide array of oils, incenses, candles, gris-gris bags, rare books, and much more. There are also a number of working Voodoo altars around the shop. Claudia has been a French Quarter fixture since Starling opened in 1995, and she has been featured in numerous television specials.

Starling is home to the Temple of the Altar-Native Star, the Voodoo temple over which Claudia presides as priestess. The temple is designed for learning, welcoming curious observers and new practitioners to the public rituals held in the beautiful historic courtyard behind Starling.

You grew up in the same building as a botanica in your native New York City. How did that affect your spiritual path?

It was a husband and wife who ran it; a very sweet, very nice Latino couple. They had everything in there from little kids who were buying their after-school gum, to people like my father who wanted to buy the cheapest cigarettes aground, to the heavy practitioners of Santeria and Voodoo who needed their items. I always thought that was really neat.

I don't remember not being psychic. My parents would buy me books on psychics and the occult, adult books. They were so thrilled to see me reading that it didn't bother them what the content of the books was as long as I read it. If I couldn't understand something, they would explain a word to me, or something. I would just gobble these things up. I absolutely loved it. I was able to learn about things that were go-

ing on with me and why I might be doing some of the things I did, or getting some of the information or feelings that I got. Pretty quickly in the reading and studying, it became clear to me what this store was.

I grew up with that, then went through studies of all sorts of different occult practices and when we moved [to New Orleans], I would just call myself an occultist, or even a Wiccan. But [Voodoo] just slowly called me back, and as it called me back, people came in and needed my knowledge of it, and some of it I didn't even realize I had retained from my experiences as a kid. It was like that old saying, "You never have to look further than your own backyard for what you really need." That was how it was for me, that's how I got back into it.

What is your advice for new practitioners?

The first thing that I always tell them is to ask questions of someone like myself who knows about Voodoo, and certainly read anything you can get your hands on, that which touches you, that which moves you. A lot of it is finding not only a comfort level with the word "Voodoo," and being able to talk about it and read about it, but also what sect of Voodoo is appealing to you. The practices and traditions can be very different in certain ways. Some of them are much more regimented, and some of them are much less regimented. Are you the kind of person who really needs the more regimented type of ritual and enjoys that? Or are you someone who needs a little more flexibility and interpretive kind of space when you go to a spiritual type of setting?

What are the essentials a new practitioner needs?

Actually they are rather fortunate because Voodoo stems from countries and people who are generally poor, so there isn't a lot of money to buy special ritual blades and incenses and tablets. People don't have that kind of money, people don't have the access to that sort of thing. So they use what they have around them. The most important thing is to have a sense of who the main deities are, and basically you can get started quite comfortably if you have an understanding of who those deities are, first always going to Papa Legba. Once you have that, you need a bottle of rum, but it's not essential. All the deities love rum. Cigars; all of the deities love cigar smoke. They love all sorts of things that humans love.

In order to start practicing, there are no requisite items that you must have. It's nice if you can afford a bottle of rum, it's nice if you can get them a nice cigar. But if you can't, they understand that. If you introduce someone else to them or if you are, for the first time, forging

a relationship with one of them or a couple of them, that's a huge thrill to them. They were once human. The thought of fame, of being known, they love that. They're very easy-going in that regard. Don't promise them something; don't say "I'll bring you rum," and then not bring them rum. Unless something terrible happens and you can't bring it, then they understand that.

It's really what's in your soul and what's in your heart. That's where the altar begins is in the heart.

You use snakes to represent Obatala during rituals. What is the significance of the snake?

Obatala is represented by the white egg or the constrictor because he will press and press and press at a problem or an issue and eke out every bit of information he can in order to fix the problem. When the various West African groups were brought to Haiti, and Central and South America, they were introduced to constrictors there.

Ball pythons [from Africa] are considered sacred in Africa. They're not that large, they're very easy to handle, they're very docile snakes. If you see them in plenty in certain areas that means everything is in balance. To see them was a sign from God, a symbol that everything was going along fine and we didn't have to worry about any trouble coming to mess up our agriculture and so forth. That's the reason they're used in Voodoo rituals. It's a symbol in our system of belief, it's a symbol of God.

We have four snakes. They love humans and they love rituals. Each one of them, pretty much all their lives with the exception of one, have been involved in rituals. They're used because they are representations of God, not because they're scary or they're meant to test anyone. You don't have to handle them if you're not comfortable handling them.

The Temple of the Altar-Native Star is teaching oriented. What made you see a need for that?

People wanted to have the opportunity to see it, and also not to feel that they had to be part of it if they weren't quite sure that they were comfortable doing that, and yet, they wanted to sort of be a fly on the wall. In some places, that's not okay. If you're not a part of it and moving around, doing the dancing or doing something where you're literally in the circle partaking, they don't give you a really welcoming feeling. And we feel that's just not a good way to really represent a religion that has enough problems with its reputation and misunderstandings about it. It's much better to let people see it and feel it without forcing them to do anything, and afterward let them ask questions about anything they saw us do so they understand exactly why it's done.

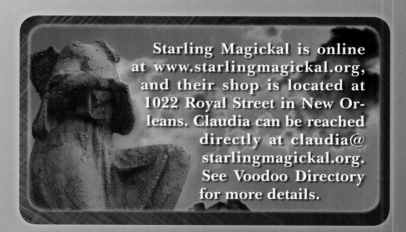

Starling Magickal is online at www.starlingmagickal.org, and their shop is located at 1022 Royal Street in New Orleans. Claudia can be reached directly at claudia@starlingmagickal.org. See Voodoo Directory for more details.

Truth and Legend

Stories about people who practice Voodoo are as full of mystery and legend as the religion itself. This book wouldn't be complete without mentioning Voodoo queen Marie Laveau, whose tomb always has a pile of offerings in front of it from believers hoping to receive favors in return. The charismatic leader of the New Orleans Voodoo community in the mid-nineteenth century, Marie is still the center of attention at St. Louis Cemetery No. 1.

Not all legends date from so long ago, though. If you've ever read John Berendt's *Midnight in the Garden of Good and Evil*, you're familiar with the role that Voodoo priestess Minerva played in the trial of Savannah resident John Williams. Although some Savannah residents question the validity of several claims made in the book, Minerva's work is indisputable.

Whether it's a legendary leader or a morality tale, Voodoo has plenty of notable figures.

Marie Laveau

Marie Laveau, the "Voodoo Queen of New Orleans," is easily the most famous Voodoo practitioner in the United States, past or present. The legendary New Orleans Voodoo priestess died over a century ago, yet French Quarter shops are named after her, altars are dedicated to her, and, more than anything else, believers still petition her for help.

Despite her fame, many details about Marie's life are based on speculation and legend. She was born about 1796 as a free mulatto, the term for a child born with both African and European blood. She married Jacques Paris, but he died in 1825 and Marie inherited another title: The Widow Paris.

The next man to play a major role in Marie's life was Louis Christophe de Glapion, a white man. Because interracial marriages were illegal, Marie and Louis entered a placage arrangement. At that time, many white men of wealth and high social standing married for political and financial reasons. It was socially acceptable for these married white men to court a woman of color—a woman who he wanted to be with for love. There was a formal process required for a man entering a placage arrangement: He had to apply to the woman's guardian for permission, and he had to prove that he had the financial means to purchase a house for his love. If the family agreed, the woman would have her own household, money, and servants. The two people would be bound to each other in every way except by law. In fact, the man would see to it that any children resulting from the union would receive proper care, as well.

In Louis de Glapion's case, there were a lot of little ones to care for: Marie gave birth to fifteen children.

Caring for that many children might seem like enough of a challenge in itself, but Marie also worked as a hairdresser. While tending to her high-society clients, she would hear about their struggles, their desires and the challenges of being part of New Orleans elite society. Marie began to make custom gris-gris bags and other works for her clients, and her Voodoo business was born. Although it was her religion, Marie was also adept at making Voodoo a business and a valued form of entertainment.

Marie was, without a doubt, a charismatic woman who knew how to draw attention. Crowds flocked to the Voodoo dancing she coordinated each week in Congo Square, and stories circulated about rituals in the courtyard of her French Quarter home. Marie used a snake named Zombi in her ceremonies, dancing with the creature in order to channel energy that aided possession.

Marie was also a practicing Catholic, and she promoted the association between the loa and the saints. Perhaps most importantly, Marie is credited with standardizing a lot of the dolls, materials, and rituals still used today.

Laveau Landmarks

Don't Miss These Sights if You Visit New Orleans!

Congo Square

Located just outside the French Quarter in Louis Armstrong Park, this open square near the intersections of North Rampart Street and Orleans Avenue is where black slaves used to gather on Sundays to perform rituals. Many onlookers would come to watch the dancing and chanting, beginning the city's long fascination with Voodoo.

Marie Laveau's Tomb

Take one step inside St. Louis Cemetery No. 1 and you'll understand why cemeteries in New Orleans are called "cities of the dead." The narrow walks meander past above-ground tombs, and it's easy to feel like you're in another world. Located on Basin Street at the corner of St. Louis Street,

A visitor leaves three pennies and knocks three times at Marie Laveau's tomb.

the cemetery lies just outside the edge of the French Quarter.

Finding Marie Laveau's tomb (allegedly: in fact, it's believed that Marie II is the one interred there) isn't easy, even though it's close to the entrance. Walk straight through the gate, passing three tombs on your left before turning left onto an alley. The tall, narrow tomb is ahead on your left, and you'll recognize it by the Xs scrawled all over the exterior and the pile of offerings on the ground in front. Instead of drawing three Xs, knock three times on the tomb while making a wish. Leave an offering, such as three pennies, to entice Marie to grant your wish.

Although Marie died in 1881, having lived to about eighty-seven years old, her fame continued to spread. She was succeeded by a Voodoo queen named Marie II, whom many believe was her daughter. There does, however, seem to be a possibility that Marie II was simply an astute businesswoman who wanted to cash in on the name recognition. Over the years, many of the details about Marie I and Marie II have blended, sometimes making it difficult to separate the two identities.

Marie II rests in the Paris family tomb in St. Louis Cemetery No. 1, the oldest existing cemetery in New Orleans. The crumbling city of the dead sits just outside the French Quarter, and tourists today flock to the cemetery for the chance to see Marie Laveau's resting place. They assume that the Voodoo matriarch rests in the Paris tomb along with Marie II, though in fact it's believed the elder Marie lies at rest elsewhere.

Whatever the truth, tourists and believers alike draw three "X" marks on the Paris tomb while asking for a favor from Marie. The towering white walls of the tomb are covered in the marks, and now tour guides encourage visitors to simply knock three times. Leaving three pennies or some other small offering is also a way to attain help from the Voodoo queen. Offerings are piled at the ground in front of the tomb, ranging from money and liquor to Mardi Gras beads, pens, and other small trinkets.

The fascination with Marie Laveau is not a recent phenomenon. In fact, someone calling themselves Marie III made a brief appearance in the 1950s. It is likely that we will never be able to entirely separate the fact from the legend surrounding Marie. But with her penchant for the dramatic and her savvy business acumen, that's probably just how Marie Laveau would have wanted it.

Statue of St. Expedite

A statue of St. Expedite sits in Our Lady of Guadalupe, a Catholic church at 411 North Rampart Street. If that saint is unfamiliar to you, don't be surprised. Legend holds that the statue arrived with only the word "Expedite" stenciled on the shipping crate, so that became her name. Today, if you make a wish at Marie Laveau's tomb and need it granted in a hurry, you can ask St. Expedite for help. Place an offering of pound cake at the statue's feet and ask for her help in rushing your request.

Voodoo in Savannah

Voodoo flourishes in the southeast, especially through the coastal low country of Georgia and South Carolina. Much of the Voodoo there has strong hoodoo ties, and titles like "root doctor" and "root worker" are typical, rather than the more traditional houngan or mambo.

None of the Voodoo practitioners in the low country are as famous as "Minerva," the Voodoo priestess hired by Jim Williams, an antiques dealer and prominent member of Savannah, Georgia, society. Williams was accused of murder, and decided to recruit his friend Minerva to help him avoid conviction. (The case is documented in the book *Midnight in the Garden of Good and Evil* by John Berendt.)

Carrying nine dimes and a jar of rainwater "that ain't run through no pipe," Williams drove to Minerva's home in Beaufort, South Carolina, with Berendt in tow.

The trio went to the local graveyard, where Minerva got to work at the grave of her common-law husband, Dr. Buzzard. He had been the area's most powerful root doctor in his lifetime, and apparently still had a lot of pull, even in death. While Williams buried the dimes and sprinkled water over them, Minerva instructed him to think good things about the man he was accused of murdering, a young associate of Williams's named Danny Hansford.

While Williams did his part, Minerva did hers, using various roots and other objects while she spoke to Dr. Buzzard. According to her, "the half hour before midnight is for doin' good. The half hour after midnight is for doin' evil." Obviously, Minerva's practice varied greatly from traditional Voodoo: she had no qualms about lingering after midnight to work on a hex against the D.A. in the murder trial.

The drama and colorful characters in Berendt's book feel almost like a work of fiction, but Minerva was very real. Her real name was Valerie Fennel Aiken Boles, and she was, indeed, a very interesting character. She rarely allowed her photo to be taken, fearing that people would use the image to work magic against her. Boles was also reluctant to touch people because that contact could be used in a similar way. She dished out the hexes, so she well knew what could be directed back at her.

Boles died in May of 2009, nearly thirty years after she had been hired by Williams to work her magic at midnight. And did her brand of Voodoo work? Williams was eventually acquitted of the murder, so I'll leave it up to you to decide.

Robert Johnson at the Crossroads

The devil and the crossroads have long been linked in Southern culture. The legend says that a young man from Mississippi went to a deserted crossroads at midnight, carrying only his guitar. The devil met him there and taught the man to play his guitar in exchange for his soul. The newfound talent catapulted that man to blues legend status. His name? Robert Johnson.

That legend has spawned many more stories about meeting the devil at the crossroads, whether it's to ask a favor or to barter for someone's soul. And the theme of selling your soul to the devil in exchange for talent is the basis of the Charlie Daniels Band's classic "The Devil Went Down to Georgia."

As it turns out, though, it wasn't the devil that Robert Johnson (some say it was actually his contemporary Tommy Johnson) met that night at the crossroads. It was Papa Legba.

I was surprised when the story about the 1930s blues singer came up during a conversation with Baba Omigbemi Olumaki of Oshun's Botanica. "But I thought that was a story about the devil?" I asked.

In fact, the story of heading to the crossroads to ask for favors stems from Voodoo believers asking the guardian of the crossroads, Papa Legba, for help. In its original form, the story about Johnson says that he pleaded with Legba, offering to honor the spirit through his music in exchange for unmatched talent.

Legba made good on his end of the deal, giving Johnson unparalleled skills with his guitar and the fame that came as a result. Johnson, however, grew proud and never paid homage to Legba in his songs, as promised.

Johnson died at the young age of twenty-seven, in the prime of his life and fame. Perhaps it was because he didn't hold up his end of the deal with Papa Legba.

Baba Omigbemi Olumaki uses the tale to teach the importance of following through with offerings and promises to the loa. "You don't go into this thing looking at it like 'I'm going to go in and have power over people,' because the people who do that end up like Robert Johnson," he says. "It's not a thing where you can take advantage of it. There has to be a balance."

What About Zombies, Anyway?

> "Any zombies out there?"
> "Don't say that!"
> "What?"
> "That!"
> "What?"
> "The zed-word. Don't say it!"
> —Simon Pegg and Nick Frost, *Shaun of the Dead*

If you tell your friends that you're reading up on Voodoo, you'll inevitably be asked if you know how to turn someone into a zombie. Before we delve into that secret, it's important to understand just what a zombie really is.

As with many things Voodoo, that's easier said than done.

Zombies are more popular than ever in pop culture, thanks in large part to Hollywood. New zombie movies come out every year, horror enthusiasts organize "zombie invasions" in their communities (in which participants dress up as zombies and go out to "mingle" with the general populace), and now, even literature is experiencing a plague of zombies: Books like *World War Z* and *Pride and Prejudice and Zombies* have brought the living dead to the New York Times Bestseller list.

The zombies portrayed on the big screen are always in search of brains (they're a hungry lot), and victims become zombies, too, after being bitten. When it comes to the zombies of Voodoo, there are significant differences: there are no hordes of the walking dead, zombies aren't hungering for your brain, and biting isn't going to transfer the condition.

But rest assured, zombies are cause for real fear among Haitian Voodoo practitioners. Documented accounts of zombies have occurred right up through modern times, although there are a number of theories about how zombies are made in the first place.

Origins of the Zombie

For devout Voodoo practitioners in Haiti, zombies are the result of magic worked by a bokor, a Voodoo sorcerer. Bokors are generally outcasts and, while they might have the power of a houngan, they have none of the respect or goodwill.

Bokors most often create zombies to serve as forced labor. They cause a person to die, then bring them back to life after burial as a mindless, subservient creature. There are many stories of people who died (or seemed to, anyway), only to turn up months or even years later working on a plantation. Zombies are cheap labor, after all.

In some lore, the bokor lays exotic poisons on a victim's doorstep. Because the victim will likely be barefoot in his home, the magic seeps into his body through the soles of his feet. The victim dies and is buried. Three days later, the bokor appears at the gravesite, where he says an incantation and cries the victim's name three times to resurrect the deceased as a zombie. (Wand, 2004, 9)

While the power of the bokor certainly seems like magic, a closely-guarded retinue of drugs seems to be the most likely explanation for zombification. A bokor makes a "coup pudre," or zombie powder, which is administered to the victim to create a state of living death. The victim's heartbeat slows and his breathing becomes so shallow that everyone thinks he is dead. Later, once the victim has been buried, the bokor digs up the coffin under cover of darkness and takes the body to a plantation or other location where he can sell the newly made zombie as cheap labor. The zombie powder is still given to the zombie in small doses, keeping him sedate but conscious.

The fascination with zombies is so strong that even Harvard commissioned a study of the phenomenon. They sent researcher Wade Davis to Haiti as part of the Harvard Zombie Project. Davis's findings back up the theory that drugs are responsible for making zombies.

Davis wrote about his findings and experiences in his book, *The Serpent and the Rainbow*, which debuted in 1985. A movie was later made out of the book, but the two are very different from each other, thanks to Hollywood's creative liberties. Davis later wrote a second book, *Passage of Darkness*, that outlines the mysterious case of Clairvius Narcisse. After his apparent death several years earlier, the Haitian man reappeared in his village in 1980, to the mixed delight and confusion of his family. It appeared that Narcisse was transformed into a zombie by drugs, but he made his escape when the drugs wore off and he resumed a sense of awareness.

Fascinated by his findings, Davis brought some alleged zombie powder home from Haiti. He turned the mysterious concoction over to a scientist, who administered the powder to lab rats. Davis claims that the lab rats were effectively turned into zombies: their heart rate slowed so much it was virtually undetectable.

Writer Zora Neale Hurston covered the subject of zombies in 1938 when she profiled the case of a young girl who died in 1909. Five years after her death, some of the girl's former friends claimed they had spied her sitting in the window of a house in Port-au-Prince. The family dug up the grave, but the skeleton inside was too tall to be the little girl's: Someone had taken her body and put in a replacement. (Wand, 2004, 45)

Other theories that attempt to explain zombie sightings include mental deficiency and catatonic schizophrenia. Certainly, the idea of catatonic schizophrenics wandering around Haiti doesn't adequately explain the number of recorded zombie accounts. The theory that proud families hid away mentally disabled relatives makes more sense. In the not-so-distant past, someone might be sequestered away in a hospital or a back room of the home because of a mental condition. The easiest way for a family to explain that person's sudden disappearance was to claim that he had died. The lie works only until the hidden person escapes, prompting reports of a zombie returned from the grave.

How to Spot a Zombie

Some Haitians believe that just looking at a zombie is enough to turn them into a zombie themselves, but if you subscribe to the belief that zombies are made through drugs instead of magic, then you don't need to worry about catching the condition yourself.

If you do happen to run into someone who seems suspicious, here are some things to look for to determine if you're actually talking to a zombie:

- The eyes are unfocused and don't fix on anything
- The face has a slack, vacant expression
- The person has no memory of his past
- The person is disoriented and unaware of where he is

Only You Can Prevent Zombies!

With such pitiful characteristics, it's easy to see why Haitian Voodoo practitioners fear becoming a zombie. Unlike Hollywood's representation, the zombies are the real victims. Luckily, there are precautions you can take to make sure a bokor doesn't resurrect your loved ones as zombies:

- Bury the body below solid concrete or large stones so it can't climb out of the grave
- Bury the body face down and stuff its mouth so it can't answer the bokor's call
- Include sesame seeds in the coffin, so the zombie will get distracted by trying to count them and won't leave the grave
- Dig the grave in a busy area so that it is always watched
- Guard the grave until the body has had time to decompose
- Shoot the body in the head to make sure it's really dead

Zombie Repellent

If you should be so unfortunate as to cross paths with a zombie, the best way to repel it is to throw salt in its eyes. Haitian legend says this will cause the zombie to disappear, or at least render it harmless. On the practical side, if a zombie is a living person (albeit under the influence of strong drugs), salt in the eyes is going to hurt and will definitely be a deterrent. Even if you're not a zombie, a few grains of salt in your eyes is probably painful and distracting. I don't recommend testing the theory on yourself, or anyone else.

The Secret to Creating Your Own Zombie

What's that? You want to turn your boyfriend into a zombie? You might want to think twice about that. In fact, the Haitian penal code even mentions that it is illegal to use drugs to put someone into a death-like state. If that's not bad enough, the drugs used to make zombies often cause serious mental and physical damage, and in the wrong amounts they can cause death.

While the zombie powder administered to victims includes many elements, there are two poisons that are said to induce a catatonic state. One of those poisons is tetrodotoxin, which is found in the puffer fish. This "secret ingredient" is the one referenced by Wade Davis in *The Serpent and the Rainbow.*

Another possible zombie-maker is a flower from the datura plant. In small doses, the datura flower causes hallucinations and is sometimes used in initiation rituals. A larger dose is used in zombie powder, which is mixed into the intended victim's food. That person will grow apathetic, shed weight, and lose his hair before finally entering a catatonic state so deep that he appears to be dead. (Gersi, 1991, 171)

After their apparent death, the victim is buried, only to be dug up a few days later by the bokor responsible for making the zombie. Once the zombie has emerged from the grave, the original zombie powder wears off, and smaller doses of the powder, or a similar drug, are administered daily to keep the victim complacent. If the original zombie powder didn't cause brain damage, the continued ingestion of poisons will likely do it.

Vampires and Werewolves, Too!

I've long had a fascination with vampires, largely because legends about them seem to exist in every culture. In Haiti, vampires and werewolves are both a part of the supernatural world, and the legends there reflect the influence of Voodoo beliefs.

Vampire stories are tied to secret sects that practice black magic, and those sects stray far from true Voodoo. The transformation to vampire is more of a spiritual one, and those who consider themselves vampires don't necessarily drink human blood: Sometimes they just "drink" the life force of other humans. Either way, you wouldn't want to encounter one.

Werewolves are believed to be created by bokors, who can turn themselves, their initiates, or their victims

Similar to a werewolf, the rougarou takes the form of an alligator. This bayou legend can be found at the New Orleans Historic Voodoo Museum.

into animals through rituals and the power of various loa. Accounts say that werewolves walk on two feet like a man, but they are covered in long, dark fur and have a long tail. The head looks like that of a large dog, and the eyes emanate a red glow. Werewolves will attack and kill people, and the best way to kill a werewolf is to drive a stake shaped like a crucifix through its heart. (Gersi, 1991, 189)

DIY Voodoo

Are you ready to try some Voodoo rituals and spells of your own? Before you get started, there are a few important things you need to know. The individual practice of Voodoo isn't mired by strict rules, but there are some things you need to incorporate into your rituals and spells to make sure they are at their most effective. You want the loa to hear your call for help, and to send you a favorable answer. To ensure that happens, you'll need a few tools and, even more importantly, the right mindset.

These Are Just Guidelines

The Voodoo experience is different for everyone. The way you communicate with the loa might be very different from the way another practitioner does. While Voodoo can adhere to structured rituals in some communities, especially in Haiti, as an individual practitioner you can tailor your rituals and spells as you (and the loa) like.

The rituals and spells listed in this book aren't the only way to do things. You can change them, add to them, or even make up your own to suit your needs. Voodoo is much like Wicca in that the most powerful magic comes from your own creations.

There are only two things that really matter when you approach the loa: pure intentions and deep respect for the spirits.

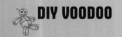

Voodoo Priestess Anna of Erzulie's takes things one step further by describing the loa in a much more personal way. "Just because *my* spirits really enjoy how we make things on their behalf and the offerings *we* give them, doesn't mean *yours* will," she explains. "Everybody has different spirits. My spirits love fried, fattening, alcoholic libations. That doesn't mean your spirits are going to resonate with that. They might just like fresh-cut flowers or Coca-Cola. At the end of the day, it's your connection with the divine that evolves and pushes you and incorporates them into your life, not my rule book on the divine. If your Erzulie Freda wants cherry soda, get it for her! Mine prefers French champagne. It doesn't mean yours does."

An altar to Erzulie Freda inside Erzulie's in New Orleans. The image on the front is Erzulie's vévé.

I had a difficult time understanding this until I thought of it in the most mundane way. I have a friend who is notorious for having a stash of Oreos at all times. When I'm with him, I love dunking some cookies in milk. When I hang out with another friend, on the other hand, we usually wind up grabbing a beer. So, I prefer Oreos from one person and beer from another. In just the same way, a loa's taste can vary depending on the one making the offerings. Tapping into your intuition may take some time, so feel free to make offerings based on the suggestions in this book.

Anna succinctly sums up the importance of letting your loa guide you, rather than adhering to someone else's rules. "I really encourage that individual relationship with the divine because at the end of the day, that is all you're going to be answering to: you, God, your ancestors, and your spirits, and that's it. No other human is going to tell you how to connect to your spiritual energies and loa, or other deities, or God, or whatever path you're working with."

Voodoo Authentica of New Orleans Cultural Center and Collection is a great learning place for people who are new to Voodoo. Owner Brandi Kelley is always willing to answer questions, whether it's by e-mail, phone, or in person. When it comes to which loa you invoke, how you honor them, and conducting effective rituals, she stresses that you should listen to your instincts. "Make sure your own experience is genuine for you and right for you," Brandi says. "If you count on someone else's opinion, you'll get confused. It's about finding and trusting your own relationship with spirit."

A Word of Caution

In Voodoo, it's not uncommon to hear someone say, "Be careful what you ask for." When you undertake these rituals and spells, make sure you have a clear idea of what you want, and be sure that you really want it. If you and your lover have split up, are you sure you want to do a spell to bring the two of you back together? Perhaps there was a good reason you parted ways in the first place.

Also, remember that Voodoo is supposed to be used for positive purposes: healing, protection, prosperity, love, and clarity. You should not be working malicious magic against anyone. If you do, beware!

> The bad things you send out will come back to you in one way or another. Buddhists call it karma, Wiccans call it the law of three, Christians call it the Golden Rule.
>
> If you use Voodoo in a way that will affect someone else, make sure you do it with care and pure intentions.

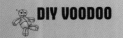

Before You Begin

Practicing Voodoo shouldn't drain your bank account. Most of the items you'll need are inexpensive, and chances are good you'll have some of the items on hand already. You can always feel free to repurpose things, too, such as using a worn-out garment as material for a gris-gris bag.

The single most important thing you need before you begin doesn't cost anything at all: an open mind. You should approach any of the rituals or spells you perform with the belief that it will work. You carry a lot of power within you, and for a spell to work, that power needs to be properly focused. One way to ensure open-mindedness is to take a cleansing bath. You can buy spiritual cleansing soaps or add cleansing herbs and oils to the water. While you bathe, ask for your preconceptions to be washed away.

There are a number of items that you will frequently use. If you focus on love spells, you'll want to keep a supply of red candles. Are you concerned about finances? Stock up on green candles and money-drawing oil.

These staples will help you get started:

Salt

A common ingredient in Voodoo "recipes," sea salt is better than standard table salt. Ethiopian black salt is the most powerful, but it can be difficult to find.

Florida Water

This light, fragrant water is the holy water of Voodoo. Use it during your rituals to help cleanse and beautify the space around your altar. Florida Water also attracts positive things to you: love, luck, money, and protection. Although you can buy it as a cologne at retail stores, the best Florida Water comes from an occult store that crafts their own. Buy it in a spray bottle for easiest use.

Candles

You will use candles during rituals, spells, and baths. They don't have to be expensive or fancy, but you will want to use colors that correspond to the type of work you are doing.

Cinnamon

Of all the things in your pantry, cinnamon probably has the most uses. It draws money and love, but it can also promote healing. Many Voodoo spells utilize cinnamon.

Altar Building 101

The idea of building an altar might seem intimidating, but in fact it's quite simple. Having a Voodoo altar serves two purposes. First, it gives you a space where you can honor the loa by decorating the altar with their colors and favorite objects. In addition, the altar gives you a sacred space where you can focus your energy during rituals. When you stand or sit in front of your altar, you should feel that you are in a protective bubble where you are shielded from ringing phones, dirty dishes, unpaid bills, or other worries that might distract you.

An altar doesn't have to be any specific size, and there are no rules about what materials you can use. You can build an altar by nailing boards together or you can cover a box with a pretty cloth. If you want to turn your fireplace mantel or a table into an altar, then that is fine, too. Priestess Anna says that you should go with your instincts when it comes to building your altar. "Without sounding vague, however it moves you to honor that space for that particular spirit," she says.

Use the list of loa in this book as your guide. If you're building an altar for Papa Legba, use a red altar cloth since it's his favorite color. Add red candles, a Legba Voodoo doll, or draw Legba's vévé on a piece

of paper and place it on the altar (better yet, draw his vévé directly onto the altar cloth). Put some sweets that Legba likes on your altar, too. Don't hesitate to get creative. Legba is the keeper of the doorway between us and the loa, so maybe an antique key would be appropriate. Don't limit yourself to copying what others have done.

Ideally, you should have a separate altar for each loa. If you have limited, though, feel free to get creative. If you choose to use one altar, you can keep it relatively generic so it can be used for any ritual. You can also consider dividing the altar into sections, with one section for each loa you serve. As long as your heart is in the right place, you'll be fine. The loa won't fault you for having cramped quarters!

Invoking Papa Legba

If you recall, to communicate with the loa you must first ask Papa Legba for permission. As the keeper of the crossroads, Legba is the one who opens the channels of communication between humans and the loa.

Before you begin any of the spells and rituals in this book, it is important to invoke Papa Legba so you can ask him to allow open communication with the other loa you are seeking to reach. You can come up with your own incantation to entice Legba to lend a hand, or you can use this one, shared with me by Denise Alvarado of Mystic Voodoo:

> Papa Legba, open the door for me,
> Atibon Legba, open the gate,
> Open the door for me, Papa Legba, so that I can pass,
> When I return, I will thank the loa!

Remember, it is not the specific words that are important, but the respect you have for Legba and the other loa, and your belief that he is listening and will open the lines of communication for you. Claudia Williams, Voodoo priestess, chooses to use a very conversational tone when she is asking for Legba to open the doorway. She approaches him with the familiarity and respect that you would use when talking to an elderly family member. You may find that the informal invocation works best for you, too.

When you are finished with the ritual, make sure you thank Papa Legba for opening the door for you to speak with the other loa you invoked. (You will need to thank the loa you speak to, also.) Leave an offering to Papa Legba for his help, like a cigar or a bottle of rum.

Which Loa do I Need?

As you gain experience in your Voodoo practice, you will likely begin to feel an affinity for a certain loa. This loa will probably be the one you turn to for many of your needs because you have a personal relationship with that spirit.

For specific needs, choose the loa that can best assist you. If you are doing a ritual in which you ask for help finding a job, you may want to direct your request to Ogun, who assists the unemployed.

Another option is to honor the loa whose day it is. If you perform a ritual on a Thursday, you might garner the best results by appealing to Oshun because Thursday is her day of power. Use the chart and lists in this book to guide you.

Greeting the Loa

After you invoke Legba, you will need to call on the specific loa who can help you with the purpose of your ritual. Priestess Claudia uses a greeting in French, but after that, she uses a conversational style, getting right to the heart of the matter.

If, however, you feel the need to formally greet the loa you are working with, then by all means do so. You can create your own greeting as you see fit, or try something that has proven to work for others. Denise Alvarado suggests that you greet the loa you will be praying to by saying the following: "Ori Ye Ye O." This way, you are acknowledging the loa and showing respect before you launch into your request. Remember, the relationship you have with the loa is like one you'd have with a trusted

friend or relative. You wouldn't walk up to a friend and blurt out, "Can I borrow twenty bucks?" without at least saying hello first, right?

While practices vary greatly, many Voodoo priestesses and individual practitioners prefer to heighten the energy and spiritual resonance of the area around the altar by sending greetings and invocations to the four cardinal directions: north, south, east, and west. Again, there is no one right way to do this. You can have a standard greeting for each of the four corners or create a separate one for each.

The Importance of Rum

If you're ever in doubt about an appropriate offering for a loa, rum is always a safe bet. In fact, your age and budget allowing, a bottle of rum should be a staple of your Voodoo tools.

During rituals, the bottle of rum should be presented to the loa. Place it on the altar while you speak aloud, telling them that you are bringing the rum as an offering. During your ritual, if you are outdoors, pour some of it on the ground or on the altar itself. In this way, you are symbolically "pouring a drink" for the loa.

In addition to its worth as an offering, rum has another important purpose: purifying the area around you and your altar. This might sound odd, but Starling's Claudia Williams has an easy explanation: thanks to its alcoholic content, rum is flammable. Therefore, it symbolically burns away the negativity in the area.

To clear the air yourself, take a small swig of the rum; the equivalent of a capful is the most manageable. Press the tip

Claudia deftly sprays rum to cleanse the air at our Voodoo ritual.

of your tongue against the back of your bottom teeth, and keep your upper and lower teeth close together. (I find it's easiest to push my front teeth out, like I have a bad overbite.) Spray the rum out of your mouth through the small gap between your teeth. It helps to make a hissing noise when you spray, because the action is much like saying, "ssss."

While pros like Claudia make it look easy, it actually takes some practice. You're likely to dribble more rum down your chin than you actually spray on your first few (or dozen) tries. To see how Claudia uses the rum to purify the air during a Voodoo ritual, check out my first-hand account of a ritual. You can incorporate her methods in your own rituals.

CALLING ON THE LOA FOR HELP
Simple Rituals

Denise Alvarado of MysticVoodoo.com was kind enough to share the following four rituals. They are all simple enough that you can do them at home with your own altar. You'll find more rituals, tips, and Denise's handcrafted Voodoo dolls on her website, MysticVoodoo.com.

In these rituals, you'll pray directly to the loa for their help with your requests. If you feel the need, you can also write down your requests and place them on your altar. It's not a requirement, but if you feel that it will help you to channel your energy and make your request more potent, then by all means do so.

Using these examples, you'll be able to come up with your own rituals when you need something from another loa. Check the list of loa to find which one can best help you, decorate their altar according to that loa's favorite colors and preferences, and remember to give an appropriate offering. As I mentioned earlier, if you do your best to please the loa and approach your ritual with the right respect and mindset, then your request will be heard.

To Strengthen Love, Happiness, and Your Emotions

Sometimes a relationship cools off and you need something to put the spark back into things, or maybe you feel that it's your emotions that are on rocky ground. Let's face it: There are times we can all use a boost in our happiness and emotional stability in general. This ritual should be directed to Oshun, the female spirit of love, art, and dance.

What You'll Need:

Gold cloth
5 peacock feathers
A vase
A bowl filled with river water
5 shells (preferably cowrie shells)
5 pieces of amber
1 yellow candle
Offering for Papa Legba and Oshun

Prepare your altar for Oshun by covering it with the gold cloth. Put the vase with the peacock feathers in it on top of the altar, along with the river water, shells, amber, and yellow candle.

To begin the ritual, use the invocation for Papa Legba so he will open the lines of communication to Oshun. Once he has done so, you can pray to Oshun to fulfill your request. If you have an Oshun Voodoo doll, place it on the altar and use it as your focal point while you are speaking to Oshun. When you feel that you have sufficiently made your request, thank Oshun and Legba for their help.

This ritual should be repeated every night for five nights. Don't forget to leave an offering for Oshun and Legba each night and remember, it doesn't have to be fancy or expensive. Denise suggests that you can even prepare a small plate of food from your own dinner to leave for Oshun.

Photo: Madrina Angelique's wangas on display at Erzulie's in New Orleans.

To Promote Love

Like Oshun, Erzulie is one of the loa to turn to when you need a boost in the love department. This ritual is a little less time-intensive than the one with Oshun because it only has to be repeated for three nights instead of five. Don't forget that you can check the list of loa in this book to see what the right offerings are for each.

What You'll Need

Yellow, green, and coral decorations for your altar
Offering for Papa Legba and Erzulie

To prepare your altar, you can decorate it in Erzulie's favorite colors. These decorations can include candles or anything that she might find attractive: pretty jewelry, perfume, or mirrors would be appropriate.

After you ask for Papa Legba's help, you can greet Erzulie and ask for her intercession in your love life. When you are finished, make an offering to her and Legba while you give your thanks for their help.

Repeat this for three days so that the ritual has time to take effect.

To Gain Focus and Power

If you must undertake a difficult task, or if you have bad influences in your life that you need to overcome, Chango can give you the power to do so. As the loa of fire, Chango's altar can be built on a fireplace mantel or near a fireplace. If you have a Voodoo doll in his image, place it on your desk at work for help with career challenges.

What You'll Need

Red cloth
Red and white decorations
Offering for Papa Legba and Chango

Drape a red cloth over your altar. On top of it you can place items that you think will please Chango. His favorite objects include horses, turtles, wood, and cutting tools like the axe or machete. A carving of a horse, a branch from a tree, or a white candle to represent fire would all be good altar pieces for Chango.

Invoke Legba in the usual manner, and then you will be ready to greet Chango. Instead of using the usual greeting, Chango should be greeted by saying the following: "Kaguo Kabiosile." Focus on Chango as you ask him to give you power to overcome your obstacles. When you are done, thank him and Papa Legba, and leave the appropriate offering.

For Healing, Prosperity, and Advice

Gran Bois knows all about healing. As the loa of the Sacred Forest, he understands herbs and how they can be applied for healing. A loving, jovial loa with an infectious sense of humor, Gran Bois is happy to dole out advice, too, so he can help if you are struggling with a decision.

What You'll Need

Red cloth
Altar decorations from a forest
Incense
Green candle
Wooden bowl
Food offering for Gran Bois
Paper bag
Offering for Papa Legba

For this ritual, you will need to drape your altar in a red cloth. Altar decorations should include things that can be found in a forest: sticks, flowers, herbs, and leaves would all be acceptable. If you can, burn some incense, as well.

Repeat the invocation for Papa Legba to assist, then greet Gran Bois. Before you petition him for help, light the green candle and place it in the wooden bowl. After you have spoken to him, have a little fun by singing songs to him or dancing. Gran Bois loves to have a good time, and he will be receptive if you express your own joy.

When the candle has burned down, place your food offering in the wooden bowl and put both into the paper bag. Walk into the woods (or whatever passes for woods if you live in the city) and place the bag beneath a large tree. Repeat your request to Gran Bois, then thank both him and Papa Legba.

And finally, while the loa offer protection, they like it when you make their job easier: If you must end the ritual before the candle has burned down, go ahead and extinguish it before leaving the area. Don't blow out the candle, though. Instead, wet your fingers and pinch the flame out, or snuff the flame with a glass saucer or other similar object.

Voodoo Spells

In addition to the standard Voodoo ritual, there are also a lot of simple spells you can perform. These things are known by many names—fixes, recipes, spells—but for our purposes we're going to stick with spells because it's the more familiar term.

To Make Someone Fall in Love with You

This love spell from Claudia at Starling is one that is inexpensive and simple. Remember, magical work is often practical, utilizing everyday tools that are easy to procure.

What You'll Need

1 cinnamon stick
Pin
Pouch or swatch of fabric

Using a pin or other sharp object, mark your initials as well as those of your intended lover on the cinnamon stick. Add words or symbols that will increase the power of the spell: a heart, "love," "you will be mine," etc. Rub the cinnamon stick all over your body and imagine it is the touch of the person you want to fall in love with you.

In addition, you can also put the cinnamon stick in a bath and bathe with it. Allow it to dry completely when you are finished.

Finally, place the cinnamon stick in a pouch or wrap it in a length of fabric and carry it with you as a love charm.

To Sweeten up a Desired Lover

If you've got an eye on someone you'd like to make your lover, sometimes it helps to sweeten them up a bit.

What You'll Need

Paper
Shallow dish
Honey
Candle

Write the name of your desired lover on a small piece of paper and place it on the dish. Pour honey over the paper. Light a candle, and ask Oshun for help in attracting your desired lover. Let the candle burn down all the way if possible; otherwise, snuff it out.

Sweet Bottle to Draw the Ideal Friend or Lover

Brandi Kelley of Voodoo Authentica of New Orleans Cultural Center and Collection shared the steps to create this bottle to find your ideal friend or lover.

What You'll Need

Clean bottle
Paper
Honey

On a small piece of paper, write your name, then list the qualities that you seek in a friend or lover. Slip the paper inside the bottle, then pour honey in, using at least enough to cover the paper. If desired, you can also add other ingredients, such as sugar, rose petals, or rose quartz. Tighten the lid on the bottle, and shake it gently while saying:

"Sweet, sweet thoughts of me,
    you will think constantly."

Love Bath

To attract love into your life, you can make any of a number of love baths. The choice of oils, herbs, flowers, and perfumes that you add to the bath is up to you. It should be a combination that makes you feel good and has an attractive smell. The bath included here is just a suggestion. Feel free to change it or to create your own!

What You'll Need

Rose water
Lavender
Orange blossoms

Draw a bath and add the ingredients. For the magic to reach its most potent, take the bath three days in a row. Oshun or Erzulie should be asked for help with this spell.

To Bring a Lover Back

If you and your lover have broken up, he has wandered away, or if he (or she) has been unfaithful, this spell can bring the two of you back together. This spell comes from *The Voodoo Hoodoo Spellbook* by Denise Alvarado.

What You'll Need

Piece of paper
2 silver dimes
6 red candles
Glass of water

Write the name of your absent lover six times on the paper. Put the paper in the glass of water along with the two dimes. Write your lover's name three times on each of the candles. Burn one candle during the daytime every day for six days.

Honey Jar Spell to Sweeten Someone

To sweeten someone's disposition toward you, try this simple Honey Jar Spell from Angelique of Oshun's Botanica.

What You'll Need

1 clean jar
Photo or name of person you're sweetening
Honey
Cinnamon
Sugar

Put a photo of the person who you wish to sweeten up inside the jar. If you don't have a photo, write their name on a piece of paper and use that instead. Pour the honey on top until the photo or paper is completely submerged. You can also add cinnamon, sugar, or other sweet ingredients. Put the jar on an altar for Oshun and ask for her help in the matter.

To Attract Money

Who doesn't need a little money sometimes? Maybe you lost your job, or had to get costly repairs made to your car. Whatever it is, this money bottle from Angelique can help.

What You'll Need

Clean glass jar or bottle
7 dimes
7 sesame seeds
7 pinches of sea salt
7 nutmegs
7 pinches of green rice
7 bay leaves
7 corn kernels
Gold or green candle
Incense

Place all of the objects but the dimes inside the bottle. Place the dimes in a circle around the bottle, then light the candle and the incense. Wait one hour, then place the dimes in the bottle and seal it. Whenever you need money, just shake the bottle gently.

Fame and Success Charm

Like salt, cinnamon has powerful magical properties. It is often used for attracting positive things into your life, such as love or money. For this spell shared by Claudia, it will be part of a charm to bring fame and success.

Claudia explains that this charm likely has its origins in the jazz age of the 1920s. Black men and women who dreamed of careers in music started making this charm to help their chances. It's still a popular charm for musicians today, and Claudia hints that you might recognize the names of some of the musicians who carry these in their guitar cases.

What You'll Need

1 cinnamon stick
1 bay leaf
Red thread or yarn

Wrap the bay leaf around the cinnamon stick and tie the thread around the whole thing to secure it. Carry the charm on you, or keep it close to something that will bring you fame and success: musicians can carry it in their guitar cases, writers can put it next to their computers, etc.

To Bring More Money into Your Home

Money spells abound, and this is a simple one from Claudia.

What You'll Need

Dirt from a bank

Take some dirt from a bank, whether it's from the lawn outside or (in urban settings) from a planter. Sprinkle the dirt on the threshold of your front door to bring more money into your home.

Money Water

Another money spell from Claudia, this one is great for bringing more money into both your home and your business.

What You'll Need

A few coins
A cup filled with water

This spell is best done during the waxing moon, because the growing moon will aid your growing wealth. Place the coins in the cup of water and let them rest there for at least 24 hours. The water will then be "charged" by the money, and you can sprinkle the water around your home or business, or on your wallet. You can also mix the water into a bath.

Prosperity Charm

Like many Voodoo charms, this one will be imbued with power during a ritual. Oshun is a good loa to invoke for the ritual, because she is associated with money. Money-drawing oil is readily available at occult shops.

What You'll Need

Green candle
Money-drawing oil
1 piece of money
Mojo bag

Prepare a ritual for Oshun, and don't forget your offering for her and for Papa Legba. During the ritual, light the candle and anoint it with money-drawing oil. Tell Oshun your request for prosperity as the candle burns. Anoint a piece of money (coin or cash) with the oil and place it in a mojo bag. Any small bag can be used as a mojo bag, or you can make your own with a piece of cloth. Carry the bag with you as a prosperity charm.

To Improve Your Life and Remove Obstacles

Here's another very handy spell from Madrina Angelique at Oshun's Botanica. All of the ingredients are readily available at your local grocery store or farmer's market.

What You'll Need

3 new white candles
Cleansing incense
Florida Water
1 fresh parsley bundle
1 nutmeg
1 bay leaf
1 fresh rosemary bundle
1 fresh sage bundle
1 fresh mint bundle
3 white eggs
1 white towel
White clothing
Brown paper bag
21 pieces of candy
3 coconuts

Light the three candles and incense. Draw a bath, adding the herbs and Florida Water to the water. Place the eggs in the bath, taking care not to break the eggs as you bathe with them as you would a washcloth. Dry off with a white towel, then put on white clothing.

Place the eggs and extinguished candles in the brown paper bag. The next morning, take the bag to a crossroads and leave them there with the candy and coconuts. As you do so, ask Papa Legba to remove the obstacles from your life.

To Resolve a Problem

This spell from Angelique shows just how easy a spell can be. Often, there is no need for fancy accoutrements or words.

What You'll Need

Brown paper
Pen with red ink
Ice cube tray

Write your problem on a small piece of brown paper using red ink. Tear the paper up and put the pieces in one slot on an ice cube tray. Fill the tray with water and place it in the freezer. After twenty-one days, remove the ice cube and throw it into a fire. Your problem will melt away as the ice cube does.

Remember to always use caution when working with fire, and only light a fire in appropriate places, such as fireplaces or campfire pits.

Charm Bath for Attracting Favors

This charm bath will help attract pleasant things and favors. It can be useful for reconciling with others, getting what you want at work, and curing ailments.

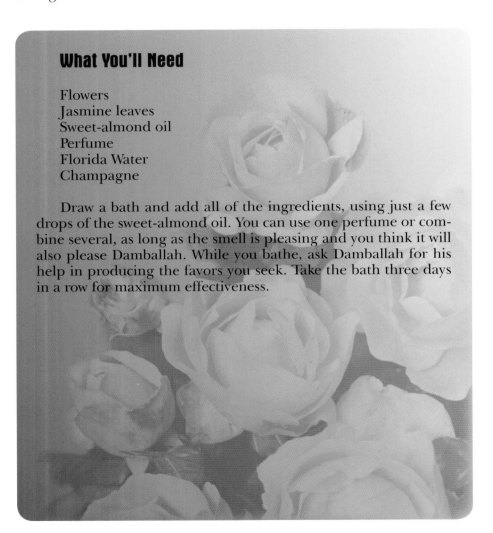

What You'll Need

Flowers
Jasmine leaves
Sweet-almond oil
Perfume
Florida Water
Champagne

Draw a bath and add all of the ingredients, using just a few drops of the sweet-almond oil. You can use one perfume or combine several, as long as the smell is pleasing and you think it will also please Damballah. While you bathe, ask Damballah for his help in producing the favors you seek. Take the bath three days in a row for maximum effectiveness.

To Get Rid of Bad Luck

Eggs are a symbol of purity and cleansing in Voodoo, and they represent a fresh start. Rituals involving healing, cleansing, and new ventures incorporate eggs. This ritual can be used to cleanse yourself of bad luck and negative energy.

What You'll Need

Florida Water
2 eggs
1 paper bag
6 pennies

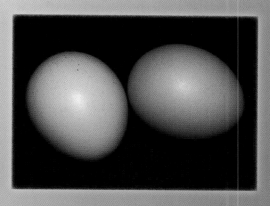

Spray or sprinkle the Florida Water in the four corners of the room where you sleep. Take the eggs, one in each hand, and pass them from your feet, up one side of your body, over your head and back down the other side. Repeat the movement in the opposite direction. Hold the eggs at waist-height and pass them up over your head to the back of your waist, and then reverse the motion. Talk to the loa as you do this, asking for help in removing your negative energy. When you are done, put the eggs and six pennies in a bag and leave them at an intersection. (Black, Hyatt, 1995, 178)

To Bless Your Home

This one comes from Angelique at Oshun's Botanica.

What You'll Need

1 eggshell
1 pinch of fresh dirt from a favorite place
7 petals from a white rose
Fine grain sea salt

Grind everything together and sprinkle in your home.

Salt Spell for Home Protection

Claudia of Starling Magickal shared several easy spells, and it doesn't get any simpler than this. For years, salt has been believed to possess mystical properties. It's considered bad luck to spill salt, and if you do, you should throw a pinch of it over your left shoulder to counteract the bad luck and to ward off evil. Salt is thought to be a deterrent for demons, as well.

This salt spell will protect everyone in your home from any physical, spiritual, and emotional dangers.

What You'll Need

Salt

Regular salt is fine, but you should use sea salt or Ethiopian black salt, if possible. Pour the salt around the outside of your home (if you live in a condo or apartment, sprinkle it along the base of the walls in each room).

Salt Spell for Psychic Protection

Here's another easy salt spell from Claudia, this time for protecting yourself from psychic attacks.

What You'll Need

Salt

Draw a bath of water that is as pure as possible and add up to a cup of salt. Soak in the mixture, allowing the salt to cleanse and protect you.

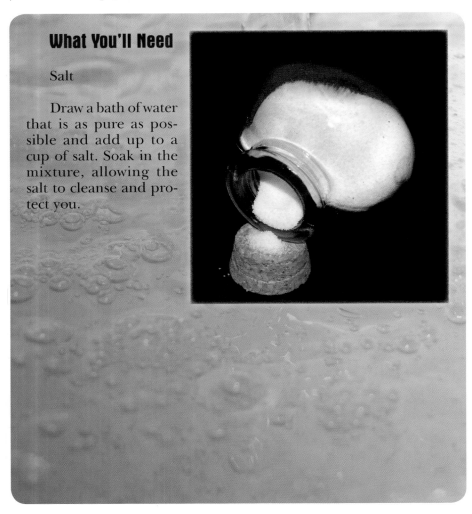

To Banish Illness

If you or a loved one is plagued with an illness, try this banishing spell from Denise Alvarado of MysticVoodoo.com.

What You'll Need

1 handful of salt
Fire

Throw the handful of salt into a fire. As the flames turn blue, stare into them and visualize the illness leaving. As you do so, repeat the following: "Sickness burns, good health returns."

If you don't have a fireplace or access to an outdoor fire pit, you can substitute a candle. Remember to always use caution when working around fires!

To Make an Enemy Depart

While true Voodoo isn't about black magic or doing evil things to others, there are ways to deal with those who would do us harm. If you want to make an enemy depart, try this easy fix.

What You'll Need

Graveyard dirt

Gather earth from a graveyard. If it is clumpy, grind it until it is powdered. Place it on your altar and invoke the loa of your choice for assistance (Chango would be a great choice, or even Ogoun). During the ritual, the dirt will be charged with spiritual energy. Scatter the dirt over a place where your enemy will walk. To increase the power of the dirt, do this for a week.

To Bind an Enemy

Hoodoo has a lot of simple spells for ridding oneself of an enemy, or to prevent that enemy from doing harm. This one secures the latter and comes from Denise Alvarado's *The Voodoo Hoodoo Spellbook.*

What You'll Need

Cobwebs
Dead fly
Black cloth
Piece of paper
Length of cord

Gather cobwebs from your house and place them on a piece of black cloth. Find a dead fly and put it on top of the cobwebs. Write the following on the paper:

North, South, East, West
Spider's web shall bind him best.
East, West, North, South
Hold his limbs and stop his mouth.
Seal his eyes and choke his breath
Wrap him round with ropes of death.

Fold the paper four times and wrap it, along with the other objects, inside the black cloth. Tie it up with the cord, leaving a long length so you can hang the packet in a dark corner of your home. Leave the packet there until it's covered in dust, then bury it near your enemy's home.

Voodoo Dolls

"Wow, it really does look just like you. Maybe, if I believed enough..."

~Matt Damon, *Dogma*

I've mentioned several times throughout this book that real Voodoo is about positive change and magic, not hexes or ill intent, so you might be wondering why I'm going to show you how to make your own Voodoo doll.

The purpose of Voodoo dolls is another one of the biggest misconceptions about this religion. You've surely seen the Hollywood version of Voodoo dolls, where pins stuck into a tiny effigy cause the person it resembles to feel terrible pain. If the pin is stuck into the leg, the unfortunate person on the receiving end of that black magic might get a leg cramp or fall and break his leg.

Fortunately for all of us, real Voodoo dolls are actually used to help people. They are primarily a focusing tool, giving you a tangible object into which you can channel your energy and efforts. Using something to focus your power is a common occurrence: Tarot card readers, for example, will often say that the cards just serve as a focal point for their psychic energy.

Some Voodoo dolls come in the image of a particular loa, which serves as a focusing object when you are honoring that loa or calling on it for help. More often, though, you'll see generic Voodoo dolls that can represent a human being. To give a Voodoo doll a sense of who you want it to represent, you can add something from that person, such as a lock of hair, nail clippings, or even a photograph. Add something of your own if the doll is going to be used for yourself.

If you are making your own doll out of cloth, slip these personal objects inside the material before you finish sewing it up. Otherwise, you can tuck the items into a fold on the doll, or pin them into place.

Speaking of pins, their purpose is also misunderstood. If the doll serves to focus your power, then the pins are used for micro-focusing, zeroing in on exactly what you want to change, heal, or protect. Brandi Kelley of Voodoo Authentica has a wonderful term for sticking pins in Voodoo dolls: spiritual acupuncture. If a loved one recently had a heart attack and you are seeking to speed their recovery, insert a pin into the heart area. The same goes for heartache or any other condition that relates to the heart. If you are prone to migraines, put a pin into the head of a healing Voodoo doll representing yourself.

There are many ways to make Voodoo dolls, but we'll be covering the most practical way here. By using material, you have the option of filling the doll with anything you want. Another popular way to make a Voodoo doll is to tie two sticks together to form a body and arms, and then wrap the sticks with Spanish moss and cloth.

Remember, you aren't limited to making one doll; chances are good you'll make multiple dolls as various needs arise throughout your life. If you are sick, you might want to make a doll filled with eucalyptus. A Voodoo doll stuffed with chamomile or lavender will help with insomnia. Use the herb guide included in this book to help you choose the right herbs for your work, or consult *Cunningham's Encyclopedia of Magical Herbs* by Scott Cunningham for an exhaustive list of herbs and their magical uses.

Step-by-Step Voodoo Doll

What You'll Need

Cloth
Pen or chalk
Scissors
Needle and thread
Herbs or other stuffing
Personal object (photo, hair, etc.)

Step 1: Double the cloth, pinning the two pieces together so they don't slip.
Note: if you want the stitches on the outside of your doll, put the wrong sides of the fabric together. If you want the stitches on the inside for a cleaner look, the right sides of the fabric should be together.

Step 2: Using chalk or a pen, draw the outline of a person on the top layer of cloth.

Step 3: Cut along the outline, making sure you cut through both layers of cloth.

Step 4: Sew the two sides together, leaving about one quarter of the doll unsewn so you can insert your herbs or other stuffing. (If you want the stitches on the inside, turn the fabric right side out before stuffing.)

Step 5: Insert the stuffing of your choice, along with a personal object from the person the doll will represent. (The doll pictured here is for healing, and is stuffed with peppermint.)

Step 6: Sew the doll shut.
While you are constructing your Voodoo doll, concentrate on its purpose to increase its power. Once it is finished, continue to use the doll as a focal point of your desire. You can use the doll in a Voodoo ritual, as well, while you ask a loa to help you with the changes you seek.
When the doll is finished serving its purpose (you recover from your cold, begin sleeping better, etc.), then you need to take out the stitching and bury the herbs because their power has been spent. As you do so, remember to thank the spirits, and give them an offering of thanks.

1

2

3

4

5

6

Voodoo Doll to Rid Yourself of an Enemy

If someone is a negative influence in your life, it's important to remove them so they can no longer drag you down. Although Voodoo doesn't promote doing harm to an enemy, there's nothing wrong with removing that person from your life.

What You'll Need

Voodoo doll
Paper and pen
Matches

Make or buy a Voodoo doll to represent your enemy. Take a piece of paper and write your petition to the loa of your choice on it, explaining to the spirit that your enemy is a negative force in your life and you need help removing that person's influence. Place the paper inside the doll, or fold it up and pin it to the doll. Carry the doll far from your home and dig a hole. Place the doll in the hole, burn it, then fill in the hole. Remember to leave an offering for the loa whose help you are seeking.

Be very cautious with fire! Make sure you burn the doll far from anything that might ignite, and monitor it constantly. Never leave a fire unattended, and also practice the fire laws of your particular location.

Voodoo Doll for Healing

This simple Voodoo doll can be applied to all kinds of healing. Remember to use the doll only once. If you need healing in the future, craft a new doll.

What You'll Need

Voodoo doll
Eucalyptus
Pins

Make a doll and stuff it with eucalyptus, which promotes healing. If desired, you can stick pins in the areas that need the healing. For example, put a pin in the lungs for bronchitis.

Gris-Gris Bags

Like the Voodoo doll, the gris-gris (pronounced "gree-gree") bag is another iconic image of Voodoo. Opinions on the proper construction of gris-gris bags vary greatly: Some practitioners specify that they have to be of certain dimensions, others stress the importance of adding a personal item to the bag, and so forth.

Ultimately, there is no one right way. What one priestess puts in a gris-gris bag to attract love might be entirely different than a love bag made by another. And, like everything else in this book, you're encouraged to make your own. Your gris-gris bag might have three things inside, or it might have seven. You might choose to use a coin for a gris-gris bag to bring money, or you might add a few drops of money-drawing oil. Do what you see fit!

Gris-Gris Guidelines:

* When choosing the color of the bag, refer to the color chart in the section pertaining to Colors, Candles, and Oils to pick a color that corresponds to that bag's purpose.

* Feel free to re-purpose material. If you have scrap material or an old garment that you can no longer wear (and isn't nice enough for charity), you can use it provided it's the right color.

* Choose the appropriate loa to help empower your gris-gris bag, and include things attractive to them.

* When it comes to solid objects, use odd numbers of them.

* Avoid ingredients that are going to go bad and smell in a short time: remember, you'll be keeping your bag close to you, and you don't want it to stink.

An Example of a Prosperity Gris-Gris Bag

While I was in New Orleans researching this book, I asked Claudia Williams to make a prosperity gris-gris bag for someone. Here is a list of the materials she used, and why.

- Red velvet material cut from an old garment, because red and green are both recommended colors for money gris-gris bags.
- Cascarilla, which is powdered egg shell. This extremely popular item symbolizes a fresh start.
- Python skin, shed from one of Claudia's beloved pets. It represents the shedding of the old self, so you'll be open to new prosperity.
- Oshun incense, because Oshun can help when it comes to money matters. Also, her incense includes a lot of cinnamon, which has powerful attractive qualities.
- 3 pieces of quartz, another symbolic item (and notice there are an odd number of them).
- 1 piece of coral, a powerful stone.
- 3 pieces of hematite, a stone that serves a dual purpose: it attracts positive things, but its reflective surface repels negative power.
- 1 Tonka bean, whose magical qualities are revered in Africa.
- A few drops of honey, to symbolize an abundance of the sweet life. Before using it, Claudia poured a drop on her finger and tasted it, then held her hand aloft to show Oshun that the honey was safe to eat. There is a legend that someone once tried to poison Oshun with honey, one of her favorite treats, so it's important to taste her honey first to prove it's pure.
- Black yarn to tie the gris-gris bag shut, making three knots to continue the use of odd numbers.

As you can see, a lot of the items in Claudia's gris-gris bag have symbolic meanings: the reflectiveness of the hematite, the discarded skin of the python, etc. When you make your gris-gris bag, you can use a combination of symbolic items and magical items. For example, your own prosperity bag might contain a coin to symbolize money, and three nuts because their magical properties are useful in prosperity work.

Step-by-Step Gris-Gris Bag

Are you ready to make your own gris-gris bag? Let's get started!

What You'll Need

A large square of cloth
Yarn
Items to put into your bag
Scissors

Step 1: Lay the cloth flat, with the right side facing down.

Step 2: Place your ingredients, one at a time, into the center of the bag.

Step 3: Gather the edges of the bag, bringing them together over the center.

Step 4: Tie the bag with yarn, being careful to tie it so the bag isn't too tight or too loose. Use an odd number of knots.

Step 5: Snip off the extra cloth, leaving only about an inch above the yarn.

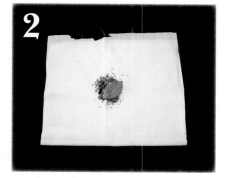

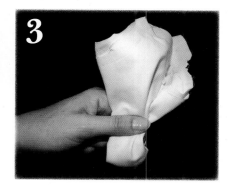

What's in My Gris-Gris Bag?

I wanted to make a gris-gris bag for protection using items that I already had on hand. White is a color of protection, so I used some scrap white cloth left over from a sewing project. It was rather thin, so I doubled the material. The contents of my gris-gris bag include these protective ingredients:

- Parsley
- Vervain, a popular protection herb in Celtic culture
- 3 black peppercorns
- 1 bay leaf
- 3 drops of cinnamon oil

Notice that I used odd numbers for the peppercorns, leaf, and oil drops. The cinnamon makes the bag smell nice, too.

I made the bag shortly before my husband went on an extended business trip, leaving me alone (and nervous) in our house. Our neighborhood, which has seen more than its fair share of crime, was so peaceful during that time that even our neighbors commented on it!

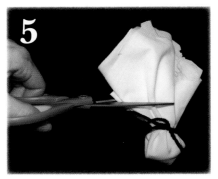

Carry your gris-gris bag with you, or keep it somewhere that its power will be most effective. A prosperity bag might be carried in your purse next to your wallet. A gris-gris bag for success at work could be put in your desk drawer.

One final note about gris-gris bags: Many people say you absolutely cannot open up a bag because all the magic will spill out. This taboo has a more practical purpose: If you open your bag, all the ingredients will be loose, likely causing a huge mess.

Colors, Candles, and Oils

Colors and Magic

Colors play an important role in all magical paths, including Voodoo. The colors of your altar decorations, candle colors, and even the color of your gris-gris bag fabric are all important.

Using a color favored by the loa you are working with is always a safe bet, and you can also choose colors based on the ritual or spell you are performing. If you are making a gris-gris bag to attract wealth, a cloth of green, red or gold will suit you best. If you are seeking love, use red or pink candles during your ritual.

This chart will help you choose what colors to use in your own work.

Color Chart

Color	Usage
Black	Release, banishing evil and negativity, self-control, resilience, protection from retribution
Blue	Relaxation, peace, harmony, sleep
Brown	Money, emotional stability, concentration, decision-making, intuition, finding lost objects
Gold	Wealth, understanding, fast luck, healing
Green	Money, prosperity, luck, success, employment, health
Orange	Legal matters, concentration, success
Pink	Emotional love, friendships, honor, fidelity
Purple	Power, success, wisdom, inspiration, peace
Red	Love, passion, sexuality, courage, power, vigor
Silver	Stability, serenity, psychic abilities
White	Purification, protection, clarity, healing, spirit communication
Yellow	Creativity, psychic powers, wisdom

Candles and Oils

Candles and oils will play a large role in both your rituals and your spell working. Use the color chart to help you know what color candles to use, and consult the herb chart listed in this book for help choosing oils.

In addition to essential oils, which can often be a lot more convenient than using an actual herb or plant, there are some pre-made oils that you might find very useful. Money-drawing oil is an aid to prosperity work, and come to me oil can be used in love spells. If you carry charms, you can anoint them with a few drops of the appropriate oil to make them more potent. Pre-made oils like these can be found in occult shops.

Practice caution if you choose to use essential oils in perfumes or baths, as some can be skin irritants. Always use the oil in small quantities if it is going to be in contact with your skin.

Using Candles in Your Rituals

- Always start with clean hands.
- Don't use broken candles.
- If you have a specific person in mind, carve their name on the candle with a pin or small knife.
- Anoint candles by putting a few drops of oil on your fingers. First rub the candle from the center upward, and then from the center downward. If your candle is in a jar, you can put the oil on top of the candle instead of the sides.
- While you anoint the candle, concentrate on your purpose to enhance its power.
- Never blow candles out. Snuff them out with a saucer, or wet your fingers and pinch the wick.

Simple Candle Magic

Sometimes the easiest things in Voodoo are the most effective! To achieve your desired purpose, choose a candle in the appropriate color for your need, anoint it with the corresponding oil, then light it and speak your needs to the loa. As you can see from the examples below, it is as simple as choosing the best "ingredients" from the color and herb lists to suit your needs.

Candle Magic

Intention	Action
Love	Anoint a red candle with come to me oil.
Money	Anoint a green candle with money-drawing oil.
Purification	Anoint a white candle with cedar oil.
Sleep	Anoint a blue candle with lavender oil.
Success	Anoint an orange candle with cinnamon oil.

Herbs for Voodoo Magic

Herbs are an essential part of your Voodoo practice. Whether you are using them in a spell, gris-gris bag, bath, or Voodoo doll, you will need to utilize herbs for their magical properties. Herbs are used in many forms: fresh, dried, infusions, oils, and incenses are all popular ways to prepare them.

This list is by no means comprehensive. I have tried to include common herbs that you likely have in your kitchen already, or that are easy to obtain. Many herbs have multiple uses in magic, and as you gain experience, you'll discover which herbs produce the best results for you.

Ingredients

Ingredient	Result
Allspice	Luck, money, healing
Aloe	Protection, beauty, luck, success
Apple	Love (especially apple blossoms), healing
Atare (guinea peppers)	Strengthen prayers
Barley	Love
Basil	Calm tempers between lovers, love, wealth
Bay	Wisdom, protection, purification, strength
Catnip	Attain beauty, happiness, cat magic, love (when used with rose petals)
Cedar	Healing, purification, protection, money
Chamomile	Meditation, peace, sleep, healing, ward off negative magic
Chicory	Remove obstacles, obtain favors
Chili pepper	Fidelity, love, break a curse
Cinnamon	Power, healing, money, success, protection, love, spirituality
Clove	Halt gossip, attract riches, drive away negativity, purification
Comfrey	Safe travel
Cotton	Luck, healing, rain, protection from evil, bring back a lost love
Cucumber	Maintain chastity, fertility
Cumin	Fidelity, protection, deterrent to thieves
Dandelion	Communication, divination
Eucalyptus	Healing, protection
Ginger	Love, success, empower spells
Ginseng	Lust, love, money, wishes
Garlic	Healing, protection, ward off evil spirits and thieves, lust
Grass	Psychic powers, wishes
Hickory	Legal matters
Holly	Protection for babies; ward off evil spirits, bokors, wild animals, poison and lightning
Lavender	Sleep, love, long life, purification, peace, happiness, wishes

Ingredient	Result
Lemon	Friendship, luck, blessings
Lily	Ward off evil, keep unwanted visitors away, break love spells, solve crimes
Lime	Remove illness and hexes, healing, protection
Marigold	Legal matters, business, emotional strength, clairvoyance
Mint	Healing, safe travels, strength, money, remove evil
Nuts	Fertility, love, luck, money
Oak	Health, protection, money, luck
Oats	Money, prosperity
Olive	Healing, peace, protection from evil, luck
Onion	Protect the home, healing, lust
Orange	Love (especially the peel), increase attractiveness, prosperity, luck, sobriety
Pecan	Obtain employment, prosperity
Peppermint	Healing, purification, love, travel, money
Pomegranate	Fertility, luck, wishes, money, protection against evil
Rose	Love, friendship, protection, fast luck
Rosemary	Purification, sleep, protection, love, lust, gain knowledge, dispel depression
Saffron	Love, increase lust, healing, sobriety, joy, strength
Sage	Fertility, longevity, wisdom, healing, money
Tea	Riches, courage
Tonka bean	Money, love, courage
Turmeric	Purification
Turnip	Get an unwanted lover to leave, ward off negative forces
Vanilla	Love, restore energy, mental improvement

Voodoo Directory

If you want to learn more about Voodoo, try additional spells and rituals, or stock up on supplies, the resources in this directory will help you continue your journey.

Where to Shop

Starling Magickal

1022 Royal Street
New Orleans, LA 70116
 (504) 595-6777
www.starlingmagickal.org
claudia@starlingmagickal.org

More than simply a Voodoo shop, Starling carries a wide array of occult items and rare books. If you want a handcrafted gris-gris bag or other item, Priestess Claudia will gladly craft it for you. There are several working altars in the shop, and it is home to the Temple of the Altar-Native Star. The temple performs Voodoo rituals that are free and open to the public, so check to see if there is one scheduled when you visit.

Voodoo Authentica of New Orleans Cultural Center and Collection

612 Rue Dumaine
New Orleans, LA 70116
(504) 522-2111
www.voodooshop.com
voodooshop@cableone.net

As much a learning center as it is a shop, Voodoo Authentica has working altars, educational displays, and a very helpful staff. Owner Brandi Kelley encourages new practitioners, students doing research for a project about Voodoo, and anyone else who has a question to call or e-mail. Also, check out the detailed FAQ on their website. Voodoo Authentica organizes the annual Voodoofest, too.

Erzulie's

807 Rue Royal
New Orleans, LA 70116
(504) 525-2055

35 Franklin Street
Newport, RI 02840
(401) 845-2055
www.erzulies.com

Erzulie's is a Voodoo boutique, with high-end products that are both works of art and useful magical items. If you can't make it to one of the shops, you can order online. The website also contains a plethora of valuable articles and guides about Voodoo and individual practice.

Oshun's Botanica

(770) 601-6190
www.oshunsbotanica.com
oshunsbotanica@aol.com

Madrina Angelique hand-crafts her items, and they are absolutely gorgeous. You can also find her products at Erzulie's in New Orleans and Rhode Island. Angelique practices Southern Hoodoo, and her items reflect that path. She also reads Tarot cards, and Oshun's resident priest, Baba Omigbemi Olumaki, reads cowrie shells.

Mystic Voodoo

501 E 6th St.
West Liberty, IA 52776
(877) ERZULIE (379-8543)
www.mysticvoodoo.com
mysticvoodoo@mysticvoodoo.com

Denise Alvarado is an artist, and her Voodoo dolls are the star on her website. Check out the Gallery for beautiful examples of Denise's art. In addition to dolls, there are also great articles, books, jewelry, gris-gris bags, and even some Voodoo tees.

Planet Voodoo

www.planetvoodoo.com
webmistress@planetvoodoo.com

The sister site to Mystic Voodoo, Planet Voodoo focuses on all sorts of Voodoo dolls, but there are other items to be found here, too. Among the informative articles are instructions for how to properly use Voodoo dolls.

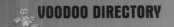

See and Do Voodoo

Voodoofest

612 Rue Dumaine
New Orleans, LA 70116
522-2111
www.voodoofest.com

Held every year on October 31st, Voodoofest is a day of education and celebration. The 600 block of Rue Dumaine in the French Quarter is blocked off, making room for rituals, music, educational talks, and food. Voodoofest is a free event and a rare opportunity to learn about Voodoo through actual demonstrations.

New Orleans Historic Voodoo Museum

724 Rue Dumaine
New Orleans, LA 70116
(504) 680-0128
www.voodoomuseum.com

    The Voodoo Museum features artwork, displays, and working altars, as well as a small shop. Owner Jerry Gandolfo is a historian and has spent years researching Voodoo in New Orleans. He offers tours that visit historic Voodoo landmarks, and you're not likely to find anyone else who knows as much detail about New Orleans Voodoo and how intertwined it is with the city's history. Jerry's account of the relationship between Voodoo and the Catholic church in the city is especially interesting.

Recommended Reading

A Guide to Serving the Seven African Powers
(Denise Alvarado)

Intended for the individual practitioner, this guide includes altar building, discussions on honoring the ancestors, and spells. This book, as well as *The Voodoo Hoodoo Spellbook*, can be found at www.mysticvoodoo.com.

The Voodoo Hoodoo Spellbook
(Denise Alvarado)

Denise's comprehensive guide captures that blend of Voodoo, hoodoo, and Catholicism that creates New Orleans Voodoo, or Creole Voodoo, as she calls it. In-depth descriptions of loa and a long list of spells are some of the highlights in this spellbook.

Cunningham's Encyclopedia of Magical Herbs
(Scott Cunningham)

This is the ultimate guide to herbs and their magical properties. The comprehensive list includes a lot of easily accessible herbs, many of which you probably have in your kitchen already.

Jambalaya: The Natural Woman's Book
(Luisah Teish)

Part autobiography and part practical rituals, this book is the story of a woman who grew up around Voodoo, and who today passes on her wisdom through engaging reminiscences.

The Truth About Voodoo Dolls
(Claudia Williams)

A compact but comprehensive study of Voodoo dolls by Starling owner and Voodoo priestess Claudia Williams. You can buy it at the shop or go online to www.starlingmagickal.org.

Manifesting Magick with Vévés and Sigils
(Claudia Williams)

Also available through Starling Magickal, this book takes a look at the power of symbols, and how to harness that power in your own conjuring. It goes beyond the borders of Voodoo, with applications for all magical practices.

Glossary

Asson
The symbolic rattle used by houngans and mambos.

Bizango
A secret society within the Haitian Voodoo community. They train bokors and are associated with making and controlling zombies.

Bokor
A Voodoo priest who practices black magic. Responsible for zombies, bokors are generally shunned by traditional Voodoo practitioners.

Coup pudre
The mix of poison and other ingredients a bokor concocts to make someone a zombie. Also known as "zombie powder."

Florida Water
Considered the holy water of Voodoo, Florida Water is a fragrant water sprinkled or sprayed during rituals to spiritually cleanse the area and to please the loa with its attractive scent.

Gris-gris bag
A bag containing herbs, stones, and other objects. Each bag has a specific purpose (to bring luck, to attract love, etc.), and is carried by the person for whom its magic is being used.

Haitian Voodoo
A religion that grew out of the blending of many West African beliefs. When slaves from varying tribes were brought to Haiti, their cultures blended. Haitian Voodoo's spirits are the loa, who are an addition to the African orisha.

Hoodoo
Although it has Voodoo roots, hoodoo focuses on the magical aspects while downplaying the religious focus. Hoodoo has strong ties to folk magic.

Houngan

A Voodoo priest.

Loa

Divine spirits in the Haitian Voodoo tradition. They are more numerous than orisha. Orisha have their counterparts in the loa, but the loa number in the thousands.

Mambo

A Voodoo priestess.

Mojo bag

A small bag that contains charms, usually carried in a pocket.

New Orleans Voodoo

A Voodoo tradition that mixes Haitian Voodoo, hoodoo, and Catholicism.

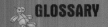

Orisha

Divine spirits with African origins, including the Seven African Powers.

Oum'phor

The Voodoo temple, also called a hounfor.

Pé

The altar in a Voodoo temple.

Peristyle

The central area of a Voodoo temple where rituals take place.

Poteau-mitan

The center point of a Voodoo temple, often represented by a post.

Reposoirs

Trees in the yard of the oum'phor, in which loa abide. The trees are honored as sacred, and offerings to a loa can be left in front of the tree where it resides.

Santeria

A religion that shares West African roots with Voodoo. It is particularly popular in Cuba and Brazil.

Vèvè

A design, often drawn in sand or cornmeal, which represents a Voodoo spirit.

Voodoo doll

A doll used to focus power during rituals and magic, it can represent a loa, the person using the doll, or a third party. Contrary to popular legend, Voodoo dolls are traditionally used for positive works, particularly healing.

Vèvè

Bibliography

Alvarado, Denise. *A Guide to Serving the Seven African Powers for the Individual Voodoo Practitioner*. West Liberty, Iowa: Mystic Voodoo, 2009.

Alvarado, Denise. *The Voodoo Hoodoo Spellbook*. West Liberty, Iowa: Mystic Voodoo, 2009.

Alvarado, Denise, "Mystic Voodoo," http://www.mysticvoodoo.com (accessed May 20, 2009).

Berendt, John. *Midnight in the Garden of Good and Evil*. New York, New York: Random House, 1994.

Black, S. Jason and Christopher S. Hyatt, Ph.D. *Urban Voodoo*. Tempe, Arizona: New Falcon Publications, 1995.

Brooks, Marla. *Workplace Spells: Everyday Magick on the Job*. Atglen, Pennsylvania: Schiffer Publishing Ltd., 2009.

Cunningham, Scott. *Cunningham's Encyclopedia of Magical Herbs*. Woodbury, Minnesota: Llewellyn Publications, 2008.

Gersi, Douchan. *Faces in the Smoke: An eyewitness experience of Voodoo, shamanism, psychic healing and other amazing human powers*. Los Angeles, California: Jeremy P. Tarcher, Inc., 1991.

Lovell, Nadia. *Cord of Blood: Possession and the Making of Voodoo*. Sterling, Virginia: Pluto Press, 2002.

Pinn, Anthony B. *The African American Religious Experience*. Westport, Connecticut: Greenwood Press, 2006.

Rigaud, Milo. *Secrets of Voodoo*. San Francisco, California: City Lights Books, 1985.

Saint-Lot, Marie-José Alcide, Ph.D. *Vodou: a sacred theatre: the African Heritage in Haiti*. Coconut Creek, Florida: Educa Vision, 2003.

Teish, Luisah. *Jambalaya: the natural woman's book of personal charms and practical rituals*. New York, New York: HarperOne, 1988.

Wand, Kelly, ed. *Voodoo: Fact or Fiction?* Farmington Hills, Michigan: Greenhaven Press, 2004.